GENEALOGY
FOR BEGINNERS

GENEALOGY
FOR BEGINNERS

Karin Proudfoot

based on the original book by
Arthur J. Willis

Phillimore

First published 1955
Second edition published by Phillimore 1969
Third edition 1976
Fourth edition 1979
Fifth edition 1984
Sixth edition 1997
Seventh edition 2003

Published by
PHILLIMORE & CO. LTD
Madam Green Farm, Chichester, West Sussex, PO20 2DD

ISBN 1 86077 268 4
ISBN 978 1 86077 268 9

Printed and bound in Great Britain

Contents

List of Illustrations

Acknowledgements

My thanks are due to those who have given permission for the reproduction of illustrations. The source is acknowledged at the foot of each plate.

I am also grateful to Susan Gibbons, Librarian of the Society of Genealogists, for her helpful suggestions, and to my family for advice from the novice's point of view.

K.E.P.

I cannot but condemn the carelessness, not to say ingratitude, of those ... who can give no better account of the place where their fathers and grand fathers were born, than the child unborn ... I could almost wish that a moderate fine were imposed on such heirs, whose fathers were born before them, and yet they know not where they were born.

Thomas Fuller, *The Worthies of England* (1662)

Preface

The first edition of this book came out in 1955, only ten years after the end of World War II and in Churchill's last year as Prime Minister, an era that is rapidly receding into the mists of history. When Arthur Willis originally wrote his guide, there was nothing comparable on the market; he was a pioneer in this field and his book, updated and revised over the years, has stood the test of time. However, it is now 20 years since he died and the world of genealogical research has moved on, while the book has undergone such substantial changes over nearly half a century that it seemed the time had come when he should no longer appear as co-author, although his name will remain on the title page. The book still includes the results of his own research in the form of the Willis Family Tree and most of the illustrations, but the text of this new edition, the first of the 21st century, has been completely revised, with much additional material.

It is only six years since the last edition of this book, and yet the changes in genealogy have continued apace. Family history continues to be one of the most widely enjoyed leisure activities in the country, and genealogical websites are among the most popular on the internet, not only helping to simplify research but also enabling genealogists to make contact with each other and share information.

The use of the internet has increased by leaps and bounds, as new lists and indexes are made available, not least the release last year of the 1901 Census Returns, which can now be searched from anywhere by anyone with access to a computer. Indeed the site was initially overwhelmed by the number of visitors, and had to be shut down for a time, but having got over these teething troubles is now operating as planned. In this book a section has been added to include advice on the use of computer software, and there is an entirely new chapter about sources on the internet, concentrating on those most likely to be of use to the beginner.

Fortunately there has been little in the way of relocation of records since the last edition of this book appeared. The Family Records Centre, then newly opened, has become a most successful and well-used first port of call for any genealogist within reach of London, and now the post-1858 wills, long housed at Somerset House, have been moved to new premises in High Holborn, London. There has also been a change of name for the Public Record Office, now part of a new organisation, The National Archives.

The proliferation of the Family History Centres of the Church of Jesus Christ of Latter-day Saints, and the increased holdings of local records in microform at libraries and record offices means that there is far more scope for researching your family without the need for a trip to London, even if you do not own a computer.

While on the subject of local research, I should emphasise that I am dealing solely with genealogy in England and Wales. Conditions and records are different in Scotland and Ireland, but the Bibliography includes guides to research in those countries.

As Arthur Willis says in his original Preface (reprinted here), this is a book for beginners, but the new Bibliography will, I hope, suggest further avenues of enquiry for those who progress beyond the scope of this book and need more specialised guidance. In the meantime, I hope the advice that follows will set you firmly on the trail of your family history.

K.E.P.
2003

Preface to the First Edition

An interest in genealogy need not be limited to those who are hoping to trace their descent from the Norman invaders, to revive a dormant peerage or, perhaps, just to gate-crash into 'County' society. There is much in the subject of interest for the ordinary man. We knew our fathers and probably our grandfathers. We may have heard tell of a great-grandfather. Who was he? What did he do? There is often little direct knowledge handed down, but, even if he had no exalted position, there is fairly certainly information about him somewhere – parish records, wills, local newspapers and similar sources. The records of his town or county may have lists of inhabitants, and these sometimes contain information as to place of business or residence. If he was a town councillor or interested in some local projects, charitable or otherwise, he may appear in the local archives. He may even be found in the records of the relief of the poor, or, perhaps, of the Quarter Sessions! A number of small details can be collected which together may give some sort of picture.

Then what about his father? Information is naturally more difficult to find as one goes back, but, even if there is little detail about earlier generations, it may be quite possible, given a little luck, to trace the pedigree back to the 17th or even 16th century from parish registers, wills and other sources.

In making research into my own family pedigree I felt the need of an elementary guide on how to set about the undertaking, what to look for and where, the ordinary difficulties likely to be encountered and how they might be overcome. I was doing the research in spare time, so anything which would save me time in investigating methods of approach would be valuable. I could find nothing in the way of textbooks, except two or three small handbooks, which by trying to embrace too much gave little information of value to me. I have found in another sphere how much a textbook is appreciated on the very elements of a subject, untrammelled by the complications of more advanced work, and I thought that an elementary book, answering the queries and difficulties that I myself had met in my genealogical expedition, might be of value to others first taking up the subject, whether as a hobby or as a profession. I have, in this book, tried to meet this need.

May I emphasise that this is a book for beginners. The writing is focused on them and their needs: the expert cannot expect to find much, if anything, new. I am limiting myself to what might give the novice a start, and am excluding any consideration of the very early times (when both parish registers and regular records of wills are rare or non-existent) and of the remoter possibilities in later times. By the time any investigator has reached, say, the middle of the 16th century or has examined all the more normal sources of evidence in the later period he is more than a novice.

Arthur J. Willis
1955

Chapter 1

How to Begin

When tracing a family tree, it is essential to start from the present and work backwards, one step at a time, establishing a firm descent for each generation before moving further back.

The tradition, or wishful thinking, of connection with some famous name one, two or more centuries ago should be put to one side until it is either confirmed by research, or, much more likely, shown to be erroneous. Otherwise one can fly off the track in many directions and be led into all sorts of by-ways and dead-ends, wasting both time and money.

The first step is to set down, in the form of a pedigree, what is already known of the family: your own name, those of your parents, uncles and aunts, grandparents, and so on, with dates and places where possible. This can be arranged as shown on the Willis pedigree at the end of the book (pp.116-22) with brothers and sisters in order of age from left to right, and wives next to their husbands.

This framework can then be filled out by asking older members of the family if they can add more detail. Opportunity should be taken to ask them to help by telling what they know. not just of the line of descent, but of the history of the family, .their work, and the character of individual members whom they knew. It is at this point that the traditions of famous connections will make their appearance; these should be noted, but only as tradition, not definite knowledge, and put to one side for the time being.

James Willis son of ... John and Mary Willis born at Winchester 28th December 1839 married 7th May 1863 at the Parish Church of West Hackney, London. Emma eldest daughter of George and Jane Ashmwood ... born on the 20th day of June 1840 - Died 3rd Feby 1910, at Their children.

(left margin: Churchfield Rd, Ealing. Buried on 7th February 1910 in the City of ... *F.L.W. ... 13/2/10)*

James Herbert Willis born at Oakley Road, Islington, London on the 4th of March 1864. Baptized at the ... of St Paul, Islington.

Emma Lilian Willis born at Southgate Road, Islington on the 12th of October 1865. Baptized at the Church of St Peter, De Beauvoir Square, London.

Marian Ashmwood Willis born at 116 De Beauvoir Road in the Parish of St Hackney, London, on the 3rd of May 1867 - Died 12th of July 1868 and buried in the Cemetery Abney Park, London.

Emma wife of James Willis died on the 4th of May 1869 at No 116 De Beauvoir Road and was buried in the Cemetery at Abney Park on the 7th of May 1869, the 6th anniversary of her wedding day.

On the 14th of June 1873 the before mentioned James Willis married at the Parish Church of Cheriton near Sandgate, Kent. Fanny Leeson Griffiths daughter of George and Frances Griffiths of Long Buckby, Northamptonshire, who was born on the 19th of January 1851.
Their children

A son, stillborn on the 5th of September 1874.

George Henry Willis, born at 12 Eton Villas, Belgrave Road, Shepherds Bush, London, (now 41 Loftus Road) on the 21st of October 1875. Baptized on Christmas Day 1875 at the Parish Church of Norwood, Middlesex.

John Burdett Willis, born at 41 Loftus Road, Shepherds Bush, on the 6th of March 1877.

The foregoing entries made by me the before mentioned James Willis this 19th day of March 1877. J Willis

John Burdett Willis baptized at the Church of St Stephen Shepherds Bush on the 10th of June 1877. JW

Plate 1 An extract from a family bible.

Speaking of traditions, one of the most common is the connection with some armigerous family, supported by items bearing the 'family crest' which belonged to great-grandfather. It may, of course, be true, but it is wise to remain suspicious of such claims; in the 19th century, particularly, 'heraldic stationers' developed their publicity, and rings and notepaper with heraldic devices became common. Sadly, there is no such thing as a 'coat of arms for a surname'; each coat of arms should be used only by the male line descendants of an individual already on record at the College of Arms as being entitled to those arms. It follows that, in order to prove a right to arms, a pedigree must be submitted to the College, backed by appropriate evidences and entered in the official records. It was in innocent ignorance of these rules that our forebears aggrandised themselves by proudly displaying the arms and crest of another family of the same name.

Of much more use in tracing your family tree are records of names, dates and places, and you should ask about the existence of any old family papers which may include such information. There may well be a Family Bible, popular in the 18th and 19th centuries, and containing blank sheets for filling in important family events, such as births, marriages and deaths. A typical example of an extract from a Family Bible is given on plate 1 (opposite). Even so, such entries may not include the names of places where the family was living at the time, and for this other sources are needed.

There may well be surviving copies of birth or marriage certificates, which will have valuable information, or even wills or records of burials or ownership of burial plots. Other documents that may be preserved include newspaper cuttings (maddeningly these have often been cut out and left undated!), letters, apprenticeship indentures, property deeds or leases, books (often given as Sunday School prizes and inscribed) and photographs. These last tend to be tucked away in old envelopes or boxes, and often the sitters are unidentified. It is well worth taking the time to show them to the oldest members of the family, in case they can name the people concerned, and any such information should immediately be written on the back, for the benefit of future generations. There is nothing more frustrating than coming across a potentially fascinating hoard of family photographs only to realise that there is no one still living who can identify them.

By now, you should have been able to add more details of dates and places to your outline pedigree and you will have exhausted the possibilities of research within your own family; the time has come for the first plunge into official records.

Chapter 2

Records of Searches

Before undertaking any genealogical research, it is essential that a careful record should be kept of all searches made, and the results, even if these are negative.

For taking notes an A4 notebook or pad could be used, and it is as well to be armed with a pencil, as many record offices do not permit the use of pen or ballpoint, for fear of marking or damage to the documents. The name of the library or record office should be noted at the top of the sheet, and each source marked with its reference, so that it can, if necessary, be looked up again in the future with the minimum of delay. If an index is being searched, or a number of years in a parish register, be sure to note down the years which have been covered, with any gaps if appropriate.

It will be found useful as soon as possible after taking notes to copy them in ink, or to type them, on to sheets of, say, A4 paper, each variety of record being on a separate sheet, so that their order can be rearranged. These sheets can then be kept in some sort of loose-leaf binder and, as they accumulate, they can be divided into several volumes, keeping some classification, such as one volume for parish registers, another for wills, and so on, subdividing them as necessary with index tabs. If two separate lines of descent are being traced (e.g. your father's and mother's ancestry) it will be found advisable to keep the records entirely separate.

Many record offices now allow the use of laptops, so you may, if you prefer, bypass pencil and paper altogether, and put your notes straight on to a computer, though I must admit that I find it much quicker to look through and organise sheets of paper than onscreen pages of word-processing, so I would still print off hard copy as soon as possible. However, that is a matter of personal preference. Indeed, a great many family historians now expect to use their computers to store and organise their research and images, and in this form they can send it to others who are interested, or even publish family histories.

Photographs can easily be scanned into a computer, and an appropriate program (usually supplied with a scanner) can be used to remove blemishes and touch up damaged areas. This has the added advantages of saving wear and tear on the originals, enabling wider distribution among the family and ensuring that the subjects are permanently identified. The same can also be done with originals and photocopies of relevant documents, including any interesting family memorabilia, such as letters or diary entries, where these survive.

Most importantly, the use of a good genealogy program can simplify your record-keeping and enable the results of your research to be clearly presented. There are many different programs to choose from, with changes being made and more added all the time. There are now well over 100 available for PCs, with others for Macs and even handheld PCs. It is probably best to start by downloading one of the freeware programs and using that for a while so that you have a better idea of which features are most useful, rather than paying for a software package and then finding it unsuitable. Comprehensive lists of software can be found on the genealogical websites Cyndi's List (www.cyndislist.com/software.htm) and the Genealogy Software Springboard (www.gensoftsb.com), which has a page listing the main features for each package. The Society of Genealogists' *Computers in Genealogy* is the only U.K. magazine on this subject and includes lists of available software and reviews of the latest versions; its website is at www.sog.org.uk/cig.

Once you have used a software package to create a family tree you will probably want to be able to make this available on the internet. An important means of exchanging information is by using GEDCOM (GEnealogical Data COMmunication), a file format originally devised by the Church of Latter-day Saints for making submissions to its databases, but now used by all major producers of genealogy software so that files can be submitted to online databases in a standard form. Your software should include an option to export data to a GEDCOM file. Further information about this format can be found in the booklet *GEDCOM Data transfer: Moving Your Family Tree* by D. Hawgood (3rd edn., 1999). The most comprehensive list of databases can be found on Cyndi's List at www.cyndislist.com/database.htm.

An alternative means of making your material more widely available is to create your own website, which can also include images and transcriptions of documents; many software packages include free web space, or it may be provided by your ISP. The technicalities of creating web pages are beyond the scope of this book, but further reading on the subject is suggested in the Bibliography (see p.107). If you submit your website address to one or more of the main internet search engines, you can then share your discoveries with others, in the process adding to your knowledge and perhaps even making contact with distant relatives.

One should emphasise that it is just as important to keep a record of searches which produce no result as of those which do. I have more than once found myself looking at something which I had seen before, because I had not recorded that I had seen it. Much time can be wasted in that way.

It is worthwhile, too, recording all mention of the family name, even if there is no evidence of relationship at the time. Unexpected documentation may turn up later showing a connection, and it may be very difficult to remember where you saw the original reference.

On a purely practical note, it is well to get into the habit of always recording dates by separating the day of the month and the year, e.g. 2 December 1839, or even 1839 December 2. This prevents any confusion between the figures of the date and year. Where months are abbreviated, e.g. Jan., Jun., Jul., keep your writing quite clear to avoid subsequent mistakes.

Important or particularly interesting evidence may be photocopied. Most record offices are happy to provide this service, for a small charge, provided the document concerned is not in too fragile a condition, and, in the case of manuscripts which have been put on to microfilm, the process is easier still, as prints are made direct from the film. It can be useful to have photocopies of census returns, as any unclear names can be studied at leisure, with the help of a gazetteer in the case of place-names. It is very satisfying to have a photocopy of a document which includes the signature of an ancestor, such as a will or a marriage licence bond and, especially in the case of wills, a clear copy can save a great deal of tedious copying of detail while at the record office.

Those interested in genealogy are normally in one of two categories: either the individual tracing his own family as a matter of personal interest and hobby, or somebody tracing ancestry for a specific purpose, such as a connection with an armigerous family, a matter of inheritance or other legal reason. In the first case proof has to satisfy only the searcher's conscience (which may vary in strictness with individuals), but in the latter it must satisfy the investigation of experts and have a legal standing. If serious proof is likely to be demanded, the original evidence of each step (or photocopy of it) should be kept with the pedigree so that it is there equally today or a hundred years hence.

It goes without saying that all new information will be transferred to the pedigree, which will, no doubt, need redrafting at intervals, as well as requiring the addition of extra sheets of paper, assuming that all goes well.

Chapter 3
Using the Internet

It is sometimes supposed that, once you have collected as much information as possible from older members of the family, the next step is to log on to the internet, and in a few clicks enough material can be downloaded to create an instant family tree. Unfortunately it doesn't work quite like that, and if it did, there would be no need for books like this!

Generally speaking, there are very few sources for the genealogist on the internet until you have traced the family back to about 1900, which will involve searching for birth, marriage and death certificates, as will be described in Chapter 4.

Having said that, it can be worth entering a surname, with the additional words 'family history' or 'genealogy' and perhaps a county as well, into one of the main search engines, such as Google (www.google.com), Altavista (www.altavista.co.uk), Lycos (www.lycos.com) or FAST Search (www.alltheweb.com), and seeing what turns up; this will obviously be easier if the surname is relatively unusual. There will be a mass of totally irrelevant links (especially if your surname is also a place-name), but there is always the chance that another person working on the same family may have a website, or there may be a link to useful references on an otherwise unrelated website.

An easier way of finding out who else is working on the same surname is to look through registers of interest such as surname lists and one-name studies. Now that so many family historians are online, the internet makes such a search a simple matter; the Genuki website (www.genuki.org.uk) has lists of surnames arranged by county, submitted by those who are researching them, sometimes with further details as to the places and dates of particular interest. A name and e-mail address are given for contact, and as genealogists are usually delighted to find others working on the same family, you may well be able to pool your information. Do bear in mind that before consulting surname lists, you should have done some basic research and know where your family were living at least 100 years ago, otherwise you could waste a lot of your time, and other people's, by making contact with families quite unconnected with yours.

The Guild of One-Name Studies (www.one-name.org) brings together all those who are interested in a particular surname, rather than just their own family, and there is a contact address for each name. As a result, you may find something of interest, perhaps indicating the distribution of a name, or variant spellings, which could prove to be helpful.

Apart from tracking down others who are working on the same surname, it is online indexes which are most useful to the family historian. There is only one major one for the 20th century, and that is the Debt of Honour Register on the Commonwealth War Graves Commission website (www.cwgc.org). It includes the names of 1.7 million Commonwealth war dead who died in both World Wars, and also 60,000 civilians who died in the Second World War. In view of the huge casualties of the First World War this website is probably of interest to far more families than might at first appear. It asks for basic information such as surname and initial(s), year of death or which war, whether army, navy or air force, and nationality; this will produce up to 100 hits, giving further details from which you can usually work out which is the correct person. You can then go to the page which contains details of rank, regiment, date of death, place of burial or commemoration (with information as to how to get there), and occasionally other biographical information as well. You should be able to find out at least a little more about the fresh-faced young men in their new uniforms whose faded photographs have been so lovingly preserved, sometimes for nearly 90 years.

Many people expect the indexes to civil registration records (births, marriages and deaths) to be available online, if not the entries themselves, but this is not the case, nor is there as yet any official plan to embark on such a project, at least for England and Wales. For Scotland, however, there is a major programme underway to make the records and indexes at New Register House in Edinburgh available online for a small charge; much of this is already accessible at www.scotlandspeople.gov.uk.

Despite this official lack of activity, the indexes to births, marriages and deaths over 100 years old are being transcribed and put online by a volunteer organisation called FreeBMD, with permission from the Office of National Statistics. The results of their efforts can be seen at www.freebmd.rootsweb.com, where searches can be made for specific events or for all entries for a particular surname. By April 2003 the database included nearly 52 million entries and a current update is displayed on the website, showing the coverage year by year, so you can see what chance there is of finding the event you are looking for in this index. As the website only includes the indexes, you will still have to order a copy of the certificate to get the information on it, but this can be done by post, telephone or fax, with a lower charge if you have the official reference (see p.17). There are also some local projects for transcribing selected parts of the indexes (try a search engine such as Google, entering a county name plus BMD Index), and a website (www.ukbdm.org.uk) which enables you to find out if anyone has a copy of a certificate you want; you then contact them for the information. It is important to be aware that under H.M.S.O. regulations, it is illegal to publish scanned copies of certificates on the web.

A useful guide as to what is available online is *Births, Marriages and Deaths on the Web* compiled by S.A. Raymond (2002); it is in two parts; Part 1 includes a general introduction and Southern England, the Marches and Wales, while Part 2 covers the North, Midlands and East Anglia. Census returns are much better served by the internet, as that for 1901 is entirely online, while the index for the 1881 census can also be searched online. The 1901 census is described in more detail in Chapter 5 (see pp.22-4). The 1881 index is available on www.familysearch.org, but the references should always be checked against the actual entries in case of errors or omissions.

The FamilySearch website mentioned above also includes the International Genealogical Index (IGI), compiled by the Church of Jesus Christ of Latter-day Saints, now including over 200 million entries from around the world and still being added to; it is of enormous value to genealogists, and can save hours of fruitless searching. There are more details about it and warnings as to its limitations in Chapter 6 (pp.30-1). The same site also includes lists of Family History Centres, described more fully in Chapter 12 (see p.91). There is a printed guide to this website, *FamilySearch on the Internet* by D. Hawgood (1999), which helps newcomers to make the most of its contents.

Another very important website is English Origins (www.englishorigins.com), containing material from the collection of the Society of Genealogists, mainly indexes to wills, marriages and apprenticeship records, with more still to be put online. Further information is given in Chapter 11 (p.82). Unlike the previous sites mentioned, there is a charge to access the data, currently £6 per session of 48 hours, but access is free from the Society of Genealogists' library and members of the Society have one free session per quarter.

There are a number of other websites which are useful for listing the availability and whereabouts of certain sources, rather

than providing searchable sources themselves. These include
Genuki, Cyndi's List, FamilyRecords and Familia.

Genuki (UK & Ireland Genealogical Service) is at www.
genuki.org.uk, and has links to other websites covering over 75
different topics, including such different subjects as Archives
and Libraries, Colonisation, Handwriting, Maps, Occupations,
Schools and Taxation, to name but a few. It is particularly useful
for its county pages, which include links to local record offices
and libraries, family history societies and surname lists (described more fully above). If you are consulting Genuki for the first
time, it is worth reading the 'Guidance for First-Time Users of
These Pages' (www.genuki.org.uk/org), for helpful information
about the site, and also the booklet *GENUKI: U.K. and Ireland
Genealogy on the Internet* by D. Hawgood (2000).

Cyndi's List (www.cyndislist.com) is a huge 'gateway' site,
with over 100,000 links covering the whole world, so once you
are used to the layout, you may find it quicker to go straight to
one of the other 'home pages', such as www.cyndislist.com/
alpha.htm, which lists all the pages in alphabetical order, or
www.cyndislist.com/topical.htm, which lists the pages by
category.

FamilyRecords (www.familyrecords.gov.uk) is the official
site providing links to national archives such as the Family
Records Centre, the Public Record Office, the General Register
Office and Scottish, Welsh and Northern Irish archives. The sort
of records you can find in these repositories are described in the
relevant chapters of this book and each, of course, has its own
website. The Public Record Office (P.R.O.) is also now part of
the new official body, The National Archives, which has its own
website, www.nationalarchives.gov.uk, with links to the P.R.O.
and the Historical Manuscripts Commission.

Familia (www.familia.org.uk) is a most useful website, giving comprehensive information about public libraries for every
local authority in the country, with addresses, opening hours, and

what sort of sources you can expect to find there, listed under such headings as census records, directories, IGI, parish registers and so on.

The Society of Genealogists also has a small number of links to other major sites (www.sog.org.uk/links.html), including official records, libraries, major online data collections and other genealogical organisations and sites. If you are not looking for anything very obscure this could be easier than finding your way through all the options offered by some of the larger gateway sites.

The important thing to remember about the internet is that it is not itself a source, but merely a tool for finding information, particularly when it can eliminate hours of searching through records or can point the way to previously unknown material. It goes without saying that all references should be checked against the original documents (or copies of them), and the results of other people's research should not be accepted without question, however reliable they may appear.

There are countless other websites, both genealogical and non-specialist, that have something to offer to the family historian, but it is impossible to do more than scratch the surface of this huge subject in a book of this size. Books which have been specially written to help genealogists find their way around the internet are suggested in the Bibliography (p.107), and I hope that with the help of them, and the websites suggested in these pages, you will be able to make the most of the huge amount of information that is, quite literally, at your fingertips.

Chapter 4

Birth, Marriage and Death Certificates

By now, you will probably have established a line of descent back to your grandparents or great-grandparents, or, with luck, even further back, but the information on the earlier generation or two is likely to be fairly sketchy, consisting of names, possibly places, and perhaps birthdays (though the actual year of birth may not be known).

The first port of call at this stage will almost invariably be the Family Records Centre, 1 Myddelton Street, London EC1R 1UW, telephone: 0870 243 7788, www.familyrecords.co.uk, which now houses the records of all births, marriages and deaths in England and Wales since 1 July 1837. From that date civil registration began, returns being sent to the General Register Office by District Registrars and, in the case of marriages in church, by the incumbent of the parish. Indexes may be searched without charge, the opening hours currently being 9.00 am to 5.00 pm, Monday, Wednesday and Friday, 10.00 am to 7.00 pm on Tuesday, 9.00 am to 7.00 pm on Thursday and 9.30 am to 5.00 pm on Saturday. However, the information a genealogist requires will only be given in the form of a certificate; when the relevant entry has been found in the index, the details should be noted and a form completed and handed in with the fee (currently £7). The certificate can then be posted (at no extra charge) or collected a few days later.

A word of warning is needed here: each year is divided into quarters (March, June, September and December), so to search one year involves looking in four separate volumes, each of which, at least for the earlier years, is large, very heavy and awkward to handle. It is as well to work out in advance exactly which years need to be searched, to avoid unnecessary effort. Remember, too, that a birth or death is listed under the date when it was registered, so that a birth on 27 March could well be indexed in the June quarter, if it were not registered until sometime in April.

The information given in the indexes is minimal, usually just the surname, Christian name(s) and registration district, so it is necessary to have some idea of the probable place and, if it is a village, the names of the nearest towns, which may well be the name of the registration district. If you are in difficulties, there are General Register Office guides listing the various registration districts, which can be consulted there.

If there is some doubt as to which of two or more entries in the index is the correct one, which can easily occur with a relatively common name, these entries can be checked against known details, at no extra cost, and only the correct certificate will be issued.

Incidentally, the Family Records Centre also includes registrations with British Consulates abroad, at which it is customary for British subjects to register births, marriages and deaths, and these are indexed in a separate series of volumes. One must not, therefore, necessarily be disheartened because an ancestor is found to have gone abroad.

If it is not feasible to visit London, microfiche copies of the indexes to births, marriages and deaths are available at some local libraries and record offices, and at the Family History Centres of the Church of Jesus Christ of Latter-day Saints (see p.91), and there are now partial indexes on the internet (see p.11). However, it will still be necessary to apply for copies of certificates, which can be done by post, fax or telephone, with or without a prior search in the indexes. The address for this service is General Register Office, PO Box 2, Southport, Merseyside PR8 2JD, www.statistics.gov.uk/registration, or for events overseas: Overseas Section, General Register Office, Trafalgar Road, Southport, Merseyside PR8 2HH. The telephone number for enquiries and ordering is 0870 243 7788. The cost of a full certificate by post is currently £11, or £8 if you can provide the full Office for National Statistics Index reference; in any case it is important to provide as much information as you can in order that the correct entry can be identified, especially in the case of a more common surname.

Finally, a word about the sort of information that can be expected on a certificate; this can be summarised as followed:

Births: date and place of birth, full names of child, names of parents (including maiden name of mother), occupation of father and particulars of informant (usually mother or father)

Marriages: date and place of marriage, full names and ages (sometimes whether of full age, i.e. over 21) of both parties, and whether bachelor, spinster or widowed, their occupations and addresses, full names and occupations of both fathers, the form of marriage and name of the person officiating, and the names of witnesses.

Deaths: date and place of death, full name, sex, age and occupation of the deceased, cause of death and particulars of the informant.

From this it can be seen that a line of descent can be traced back by means of a birth certificate, then the marriage of the parents, followed by the birth of the father, and so on, back to 1837. This is not only costly, but it also gives no information on brothers and sisters in each generation, nor on the environment in which the family was living. Certificates are best used in conjunction with census returns, which started (in their present form) at about the same time as civil registration, and are an invaluable source for genealogists.

For example, suppose that a birth has been found for 1863; a search of the census return for that place in 1861 would be the next step. If the family is found there, the place of birth of each member would be given (simplifying the search for the next birth certificate) and, with luck, a grandparent might be found living in the same household, or nearby. This could take one back another generation, and directly to the parish registers which are needed before the period of civil registration. If, however, the family is not found in the 1861 census, it is also worth trying that of 1871 or, perhaps, searching for the birth of an older child to give a clue as to the family's whereabouts in 1861.

Chapter 5
Census Returns

A Census has been taken in England and Wales every 10 years from 1801 (except in 1941 during World War II). The earlier ones, which did not give names, have not, with one exception, survived, and those less than 100 years old are not yet open to inspection. But the Census Returns for 1841, 1851, 1861, 1871, 1881 and 1891 can be seen on microfilm and that for 1901 online and on microfiche at the Family Records Centre, 1 Myddelton Street, London EC1R 1UW, telephone: 020 8392 5300, www.familyrecords.gov.uk/frc. The current opening hours are given in the previous Chapter (see p.15), as the census returns are conveniently under the same roof as the records of births, marriages and deaths.

Copies of most of these census returns can also be seen at local record offices, some libraries, the Society of Genealogists' Library and Family History Centres (see pp.83 and 91), and the 1901 census can be searched from any computer with internet access. For details of locally-held copies, see *Census Returns in Microform 1841-1891: A Directory to Local Holdings* by J. Gibson and E. Hampson (6th edn. 2001).

Of the above censuses, that for 1841 is the least useful. It gives the names, ages (within five years) and occupations of all persons in the household, but it does not give places of birth, beyond stating whether or not the individual was born in the county of residence.

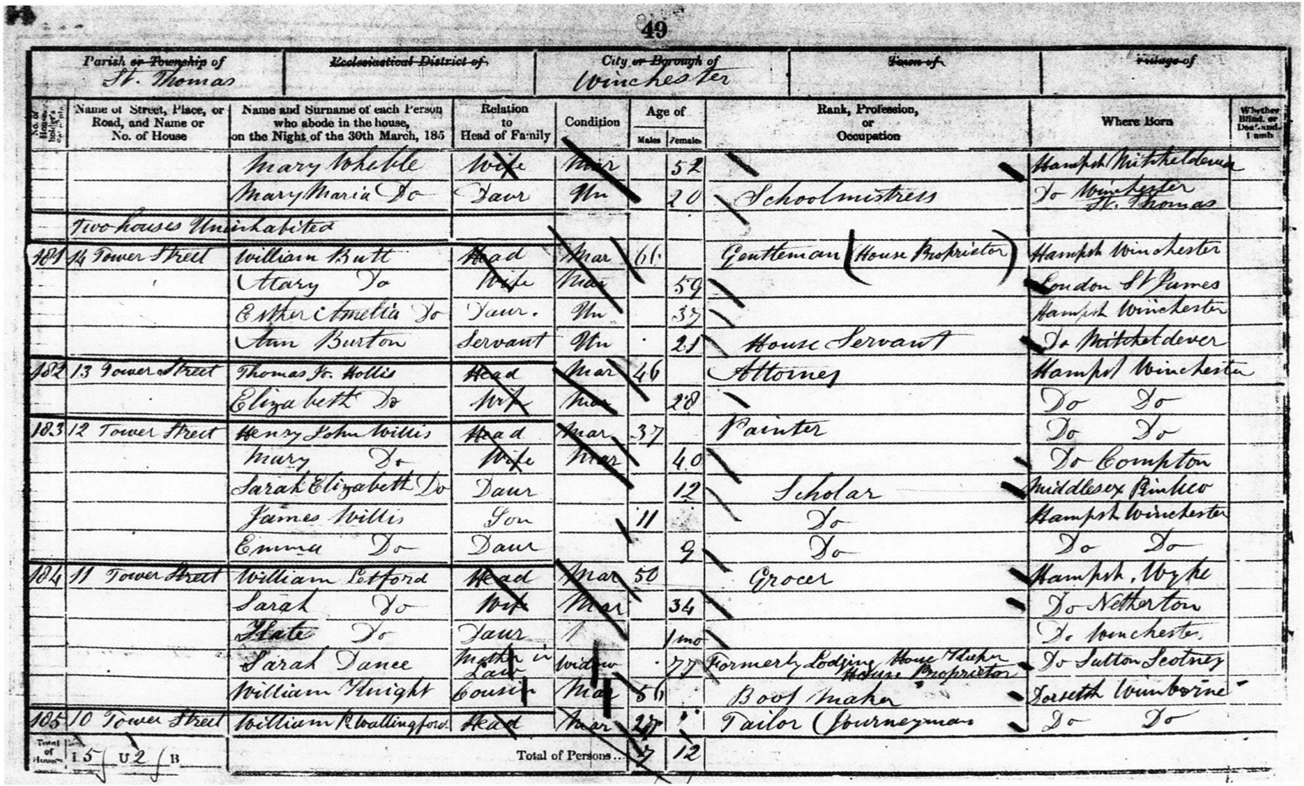

49

Parish ~~or Township~~ of St. Thomas	~~Ecclesiastical District of~~	City ~~or Borough~~ of Winchester	~~Town of~~	~~Village of~~					
No. of Householders' Schedule	Name of Street, Place, or Road, and Name or No. of House	Name and Surname of each Person who abode in the house, on the Night of the 30th March, 185	Relation to Head of Family	Condition	Age of Males	Age of Females	Rank, Profession, or Occupation	Where Born	Whether Blind, or Deaf-and-Dumb
		Mary Whebble	Wife	Mar		52		Hampsh Mitcheldever	
		Mary Maria Do	Daur	Un		20	Schoolmistress	Do Winchester St. Thomas	
	Two houses Uninhabited								
181	14 Tower Street	William Butt	Head	Mar	61		Gentleman (House Proprietor)	Hampsh Winchester	
		Mary Do	Wife	Mar		59		London St James	
		Esther Amelia Do	Daur.	Un		37		Hampsh Winchester	
		Ann Burton	Servant	Un		21	House Servant	Do Mitcheldever	
182	13 Tower Street	Thomas Jo. Hollis	Head	Mar	46		Attorney	Hampsh Winchester	
		Elizabeth Do	Wife	Mar		28		Do Do	
183	12 Tower Street	Henry John Willis	Head	Mar	37		Painter	Do Do	
		Mary Do	Wife	Mar		40		Do Compton	
		Sarah Elizabeth Do	Daur			12	Scholar	Middlesex Pimlico	
		James Willis	Son		11		Do	Hampsh Winchester	
		Emma Do	Daur			9	Do	Do Do	
184	11 Tower Street	William Pettford	Head	Mar	50		Grocer	Hampsh, Wyke	
		Sarah Do	Wife	Mar		34		Do Netherton	
		Kate Do	Daur			1 mo		Do Winchester	
		Sarah Dance	Mother in Law	Widow		77	Formerly Lodging House Keeper House Proprietor	Do Sutton Scotney	
		William Knight	Cousin	Mar	56		Boot Maker	Dorseth Wimborne	
185	10 Tower Street	William R. Wallingford	Head	Mar	27		Tailor (Journeyman	Do Do	
Total of Houses 1 5 U 2 B				Total of Persons	7	12			

Plate 2 A census return (1851 Census of Winchester, Hampshire. The National Archives: Public Record Office HO 107/1674 f44v). Crown Copyright. Reproduced by permission of the Controller of Her Majesty's Stationery Office.

The returns for 1851 onwards are more useful, for not only do they give the exact age (as alleged) and the relationships of the members of the household to one another, but, most important of all, they give the place of birth (see opposite). In the case of a village or small town, it should then be easy to pin-point the parish register. Sometimes in the case of a large town or city, the parish of birth is given. If not, it can mean a search of a number of registers (possibly including non-Church of England ones). If the place of birth is simply given as 'London', then one's heart truly sinks, as it can be a case of looking for the proverbial needle in a haystack, although there are now a number of indexes available, some available online, which can provide a lead even in this situation.

Even if you are intending to seach the census returns locally rather than by visiting London, some guidance as to how they are arranged, and how to find the entry you need, may be helpful. There is a *How to use …* sheet for the 1841 to 1891 Census Returns, as well as a separate one for 1901, available in the Reference area at the Family Records Centre, which explains the series of index binders, colour-coded for each census, and how to use them. I find it easiest to go straight to the Place Name Index binders for the relevant year, which give the registration district and sub-district numbers for every parish, village and town in the country (these are needed for the microfilm reference numbers) and include the availability of surname and street indexes for each place listed.

If a street index is listed, it will be found in the white-labelled binders for that particular year. If there are names indexes for the place you are interested in, further details can be found in the 'Index to Surnames Indexes' binders. Apart from the 1881 and 1901 censuses (see below), there is no complete index for names, and those that have been compiled (often by local family history groups) are in various forms: printed, typescript or on microfiche, and arranged by parish, registration district or county. In some cases (such as the 1851 census for Essex) even rural areas have indexes to names, which can save a lot of time in searching. On the other hand, some names indexes (including Middlesex for 1851) list only surnames for each district, so looking up each reference for a common name becomes a laborious task.

Whether or not you find an index, you will need a two-part reference in order to find the right microfilm. These are given in the Reference Books for each census, arranged by registration district. The first part is the reference for each census: 1841 and 1851 – HO 107; 1861 – RG 9; 1871 – RG 10; 1881 – RG11; 1891 – RG12; 1901 – RG13. The second part is the number of the microfilm. These are in labelled drawers in the reading room, as are the microfiche copies of the 1901 census, and you help yourself to the one you want, replacing it with the dummy box which is by each microfilm reader.

Photocopies of pages from the census returns can be done cheaply on the spot from the microfilms or fiches, using the special copiers available; if you prefer, the staff will do this for you at a small extra charge.

For the 1881 census there is a complete index to names, arranged both by county and for the whole of England and Wales, available on microfiche in the reading room; this includes age, place of residence and of birth, and name of the head of household for every person included in the census, making it relatively simple to identify the particular person or family you are looking for, although there are occasional omissions or inaccuracies due to human error. The microfilm number and page reference are given, so the relevant entry can be easily located. The index can also be seen online at www.familysearch. org (see p.12).

The 1901 census is available online, and can be accessed from a home computer (www.census.pro.gov.uk) and in larger public libraries and record offices, or at the Family Records

Centre, where there are also copies on microfiche, useful if you want to search a particular area as well as look up an individual or family. As with the 1881 census, there is a comprehensive index to names and places, which can be searched free of charge. Entries can then be downloaded either as Transcription Details (a typed copy of the entry for one person or a household) or an Image (a copy of the original page from the census which includes a named person). To view the transcription details for one person costs 50p, with a further 50p to see the details for other members of the household; the charge for viewing the image of one page is 75p. For a minimum charge of £5 an Account Session can be purchased online, allowing access during a 48-hour period. An alternative method of payment is by voucher, which can be bought at certain libraries (listed on the census website) or at the Family Records Centre. Once viewed, transcriptions and images can be printed out or saved on your computer. If you would prefer a larger copy, A3 size prints of whole pages can be ordered at 50p each, plus postage and packing (minimum charge of £2.50).

Although the transcribed version avoids the problem of deciphering the handwriting of the enumerator, I would always recommend seeing the image, in case there have been any errors in transcription. While on the subject of errors, do remember that the index is not infallible, as I know from personal experience. In one instance, not only had a simple error changed the family's surname from Stockdale to Stocklade, but one place of birth, Gateshead, had been misread as 'Salishead'. In another family (Jennings), one daughter (Helen) and one son (William) could not be found at all in the index, although they were listed with the rest of the family when the household was located through their father's name; yet none of these names is unusual, and all were clearly legible in the original census return.

The frustrating thing about such mistakes is that they can render an individual, or, in the Stockdale case, an entire family untraceable in the index. In fact the Stockdale error in the index proved to be the result of an earlier mistake by the census enumerator, who wrote the surname as 'Stocklade' in the census return, proving that human error can creep in at any stage.

There are ways round this, as the index allows searches by surname and even first name only, but obviously for this extra details must be provided to narrow the search, such as age, sex, marital status, places of birth and of residence - not much use if the last two are just what you were hoping to discover from the census in the first place. You can also try searching under the names of other members of the household or, if all else fails, it may be necessary to obtain the birth certificate of another child in the family, born closer to 1901, to give an address, or even to bypass the 1901 census at this stage, perhaps going back to it at a later date with further information to tackle the index again. It is worth remembering that if you know where the family was living, you can search the microfiche copies, which have street indexes for most towns and cities, though this is not a practical proposition if all you have is the name of a district in a large city.

One point to remember about census returns is that the information in them was supplied by the families themselves, who may have had their own reasons for adjusting an age or place of birth, or may simply not have known the correct details.

This happened in my own family: my great-grandfather's age is given as 48 in the 1871 census return, when he was actually 54. At the time he was a lodger in the household of his future father-in-law, and no doubt preferred that his bride's family should not know his true age – especially as she was 25 years his junior.

Mistakes can also be made through simple human error. An example of this occurred in the entry for a family named Lambert in the 1851 census: living with John and Mary Lambert were their unmarried son and daughter, a married daughter, Elizabeth Hutchins, and two granddaughters, both surnamed

Lambert, which was puzzling until searches under both surnames for their birth certificates showed that they were Elizabeth's daughters, and had the surname Hutchins. If in doubt it is always worth trying to find a family in more than one census return in case differing ages or places are given.

Places of birth can pose problems, especially if someone was living in a different part of the country from where he was born, and the place of birth was small and obscure. In the 1881 census the birthplace of a farmer living in Devon was given as 'Essex, Heningham' but there is no such place in Essex. Much poring over maps produced 'Hedingham' as a possibility, and in subsequent searches the correct baptism was found at Sible Hedingham, one of two Hedinghams in Essex.

In another instance two sisters from a large family, all born in the tiny village of East Harlsey, Yorkshire, were both living separately away from home in 1901 and were either unsure of the exact name of their birthplace, or were misheard - in one entry it appears as 'Yorks., East Alsey' and in the other as 'Easter Harsley' [sic], with no county at all. Problems such as these can generally be resolved by comparing information from other sources, and the use of a good gazetteer or an Ordnance Survey map.

With luck you will not encounter too many pitfalls of this nature, and it should be possible to trace your family back to the first quarter of the 19th century through the use of the records described in this chapter and the previous one. Prior to the 1830s and 1840s there was no national system of registration or census-taking, so you now have to turn to local archives, which will almost certainly in the first instance mean parish registers.

Chapter 6

Parish Registers

Until the order of Thomas Cromwell in 1538 there was no obligation to record baptisms, marriages and burials, though there are a few registers from an earlier date still extant. From that year the incumbent of the parish was required to keep such a record, but nevertheless a large number of the earliest registers have not survived. They were paper books at first until in 1597 it was ordered that they should be of parchment. Then they were apparently mostly transcribed, perhaps not without errors in so doing. Early volumes are in many cases missing, so one will face an advantage or handicap of good or bad luck in the search of a particular parish. It was also ordained in 1597 that copies of the register entries should be made and forwarded to the diocesan authorities. These copies are known as the 'Bishops' Transcripts' and should be available to fill gaps where the original registers are lost, but, unfortunately, particularly in the earlier years, gaps will be found in these too.

During the Civil War, when what are known as Commonwealth 'intruders' took over parishes to the exclusion of the regular incumbents, the keeping of the registers became irregular. In 1653 under the Commonwealth the incumbent was often deprived of his authority over the registers, the keeping of which was transferred to a layman called a 'Register'. The solemnization of marriages was also soon after taken from the incumbent and the duty transferred to the justices. It will be found, therefore, that records of marriages during the Civil War and Commonwealth are often either missing or incomplete, though fortunately the record of baptisms and burials may be found more regularly kept. The period and extent of the irregularity varies. In 1662 the intruders, if they did not 'conform', were often ejected.

In 1754, following Lord Hardwicke's Marriage Act, record was to be kept of banns as well as marriages and the register was to be signed by the parties. Books of printed forms became available for this. They are not always to be found, but should be looked for.

Under Rose's Act of 1812 the registers were to be kept in three separate volumes in official printed form, and in smaller parishes where there are few entries the baptisms and burial volumes will be found still in use to this day.

On 1 July 1837 the system of civil registration now in force began, as has already been mentioned (p.15). Baptism and burial (as distinct from birth and death) records were continued in the churches. Marriages, instead of being included in the bishops' transcripts, were returned in the standard form to the Registrar General, though they are found to a limited extent in the transcript.

Parish registers are, therefore, the main source of information for family history prior to 1837, and once a family line has been traced back as far as possible through birth, marriage and death certificates, and census returns, the next stage is to search for the baptism of the earliest known ancestor. The place and approximate year of birth will have been established from census returns, and the registers of the appropriate parish need to be located and examined.

It is worth remembering that large towns and cities include several different parishes, each with its own registers, and also that the place of birth given in a census may not itself be a parish, but could be a hamlet in a parish of another name.

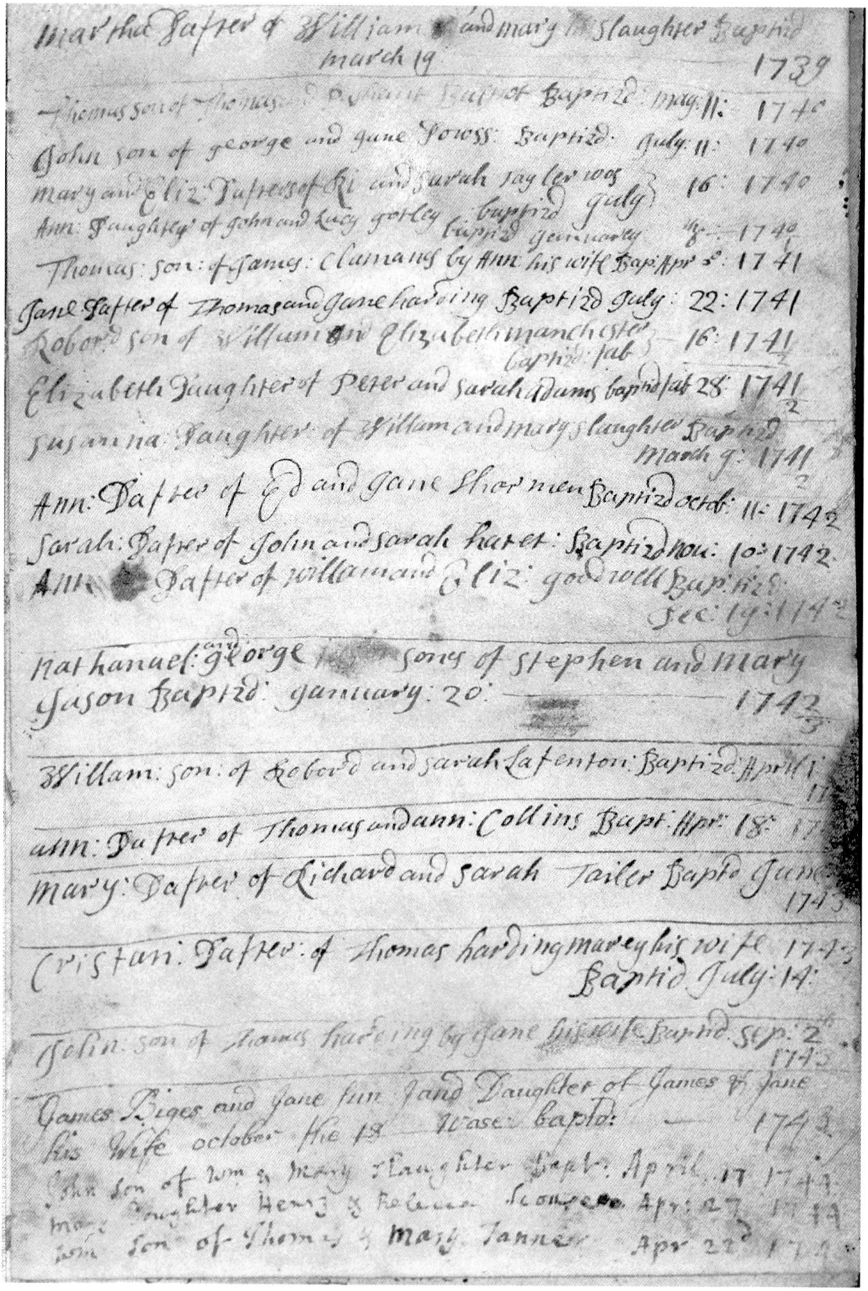

Plate 3 Entries from a Parish Register
(from the Parish Register, vol. 2, of Faccombe, Hants.)
(Reproduced by courtesy of the Hampshire Record Office)

TRANSCRIPT OF PLATE 3

Martha Dafter [daughter] of William & Mary Slaughter Baptiz[e]d March 19 1739

Thomas Son of Thomas & [names not clear] Baptiz[e]d May 11 1740

John Son of George and Jane Powss[?] Baptiz[e]d July 11 1740

Mary and Eliz: Dafters of Ri[chard] and Sarah Tayler was[sic]

Baptiz[e]d July 16 1740

Ann: Daughter of John and Lucy Gorley Baptiz[e]d January 6 1740/1

Thomas Son of James Clamans by Ann his wife Bap: Apr: 5 1741

Jane Dafter of Thomas and Jane Harding Baptiz[e]d July 22 1741

Robord [Robert] Son of William and Elizabeth Manchester

Baptiz[e]d Feb: 16 1741/2

Elizabeth Daughter of Peter and Sarah Adams Baptiz[e]d Feb: 28 1741/2

Susanna Daughter of William and Mary Slaughter Baptiz[e]d March 9 1741/2

Ann Dafter of Ed: and Jane Shermen Baptiz[e]d Octob: 11 1742

Sarah Dafter of John and Sarah Hatet[?] Baptiz[e]d Nov: 10 1742

Ann Dafter of William and Eliz: Goodwell Baptiz[e]d Dec: 19 1742

Nathanael and George Sones of Stephen and Mary Jason

Baptiz[e]d January 20 1742/3

William Son of Robord and Sarah Lafenton Baptiz[e]d April 1[?] 1743

Ann Dafter of Thomas and Ann Collins Bapt: Apr: 18 1743

Mary Dafter of Richard and Sarah Tailer Bapti[ze]d June [date illegible] 1743

Cristan: Dafter of Thomas Harding Marey his Wife Bapti[ze]d July 14 1743

John Son of Thomas Harding by Jane his Wife Bapti[ze]d Sep: 2 1743

James Biges and Jane Sun[sic] and Daughter of James and Jane his Wife

October the 18 wase[sic] bapt[ize]d: 1743

John Son of W[illia]m. and Mary Slaughter Bapt: April 17 1744

Mary Daughter Henry & Rebecca Scouse Apr: 27 1744

W[illia]m. Son of Thomas & Mary Tanner Apr: 22d 1744

An invaluable guide for identifying parishes and locating their registers is *The Phillimore Atlas and Index of Parish Registers* (2003), which includes pre-1837 topographical maps and modern maps showing parish boundaries and probate jurisdictions, with comprehensive lists of all parishes, arranged by county, giving details of which registers survive, and where, and also the availability of copies and indexes. The third edition (2003) also contains census information and registration districts.

Before consulting the actual registers, it is worth investigating one or more of the centralised indexes which cover some, though not all, parish registers. These can be particularly useful if a place of birth is uncertain.

The most important of these is the International Genealogical Index (IGI) which has been widely available for many years, and can be consulted online at www.familysearch.org, at the Society of Genealogists and the Guildhall Library in London, county record offices, Family History Centres and many large libraries.

It was originally conceived as an index, on microfiche, to the filmed copies of parish registers made by the Church of Jesus Christ of Latter-day Saints and stored in Utah. However, its potential value to genealogists persuaded the Church authorities to allow copies to be made for other libraries, the first being sent to the Society of Genealogists. The latest edition contains more than 200 million names from around the world.

The microfiches for this country consist of an alphabetical index, arranged by county, of births, baptisms and marriages but, before seizing on it as the answer to every genealogist's prayer, a few words of warning are needed. Firstly, it does not offer comprehensive coverage of every parish in the country, nor does it include deaths and burials; *The Phillimore Atlas and Index of Parish Registers* lists those parishes and years which are included. Furthermore, the entries are not only in a standardised form, but variant spellings of surnames and Christian names can be indexed in a most illogical way, often separately from their most usual form, so care is needed to check all possible variations, however improbable. Finally, do bear in mind that this is an Index, and was only intended as such, so any possibly relevant entries should be checked against the original sources, usually parish registers; inevitably mistakes have crept in, due to human error and poor legibility of the original.

Within its limitations, however, the IGI can be a godsend, especially in cases where a family moved around a lot, when a wide geographical area can be scanned in a short time. It can also be useful in tracking down other members of a family in a particular parish, especially a large one, where to search the registers year by year would be a tedious and time-consuming task. In short, use it as an aid but not a primary source.

I found it invaluable in tracing my own family, which had become stuck at Thomas Tatchell and his wife Phoebe, whose six children were baptised at Stoke Damerel, Devon (the parish for Devonport) between 1760 and 1770, but whose marriage could not be found locally. A search of the IGI produced the marriage of Thomas Tatchell and Phebe [*sic*] Tubbs in Portsea, Hampshire in 1756 and the baptism of their son the following year. Thomas was known to have been a ropemaker, and searches were made in pay lists of naval dockyard ropemakers at the P.R.O. for Portsmouth and Devonport; Thomas's career was traced, including his move from Portsmouth to Devonport in January 1758, confirming that the marriage was the right one.

Marriages from many counties are indexed in Boyd's Marriage Index, at the Society of Genealogists, which is more fully described in Chapter 11 (see p.84). This gives only the barest information: surname and Christian name of the bride and groom, and the year and parish of the marriage, so more detail must be sought from the parish register concerned.

Marriages in the London area only are included in Pallot's Marriage Index, which covers most entries in the years 1780-1837. There are no copies of this index, and applications for searches should be made by post or e-mail to the Institute of Heraldic and Genealogical Studies, 79-82 Northgate, Canterbury, Kent CT1 1BA, telephone: 01227 768664, www.ihgs.ac.uk; a minimum fee of £15 is payable. However, for this often difficult period in London immediately before civil registration this index can provide just the clue that is needed.

Other county indexes are being compiled by local family history societies and by individuals, who will undertake searches for a small fee. Details can be found in *Marriage and Census Indexes for Family Historians* by J. Gibson and E. Hampson (Federation of Family History Societies, 8th ed. 2000).

As already mentioned, all entries from indexes should be checked in the original registers, or, if this is not possible, in a good copy. The Society of Genealogists has the largest collection of parish register copies in the country, listed in *County Sources at the Society of Genealogists* (volumes for each county) and there are many printed copies available in local record offices and libraries.

Virtually all original parish registers are now held in county record offices and a few other libraries, and these can generally be visited free. In the rare instances where the registers are still in the parish, an appointment should be made with the incumbent (enclosing a stamped addressed envelope for reply), who is entitled to charge a fee.

In view of the greatly increased number of people wishing to consult registers (and other documents) at record offices, it is advisable to telephone in advance to check on the availability of the required records and, if necessary, to book a seat, particularly if the registers concerned are on microfilm, in which case a microfilm reader may need to be booked.

Unless the beginner has prepared himself, he may be disappointed when he first sees a parish register, because he finds he cannot read the earlier entries. The hands of the 16th and 17th centuries and even the 18th are difficult to decipher until one is accustomed to them. Photocopies of wills or other documents could be obtained and studied at leisure instead of at a repository which may be distant from home. A book such as *Reading Tudor and Stuart Handwriting* or *The Secretary Hand 'ABC' Book* (see Bibliography, p.108) will be found useful. Help may also be obtained from the copies of the parish register (Plate 3), wills and inventory (Plates 5, 6 and 7) and court roll (Plate 10) and their transcripts on facing pages in this book. It will be found that by comparing letters of unknown words with those of words which are obvious, the alphabet in use can gradually be built up. Although, perhaps, more care was taken in writing in the past, there was good and bad writing then just as there is today, and, even when some knowledge of the letters used has been acquired, it may take time to become accustomed to individual handwriting. The genealogist should always carry a pocket magnifying glass to help him to decipher letters which are difficult, covered by blots or faint from age.

The arrangement of a parish register will not always be found orderly. Baptisms and burials may be intermixed and in the earlier days marriages too may be found in the same sequence. Sometimes facing pages will be used as a means of separation, sometimes opposite ends of the volume (so don't forget to look at the back end!). Volumes do not usually end completely at a fixed date. If the pages allotted to baptisms are filled, the incumbent may have started a new book for them but continued the entry of marriages and burials in the old book.

Even when separation is attempted, a stray item may be in the wrong place. In examining the registers of a parish from which the marriages had been printed, I found a marriage in among the burials which had not been found by the editor of the printed volume. A series of pages which appears to be blank should be carefully examined. It may be that two or three pages in the middle have been used.

One must remember, too, that the registers were sometimes kept on loose sheets which were bound up afterwards, when the sheets may have been sewn up in the wrong order. If there is no date at the top of the page, this may be very confusing. Pages should be checked to see that they are in proper serial order. It was not uncommon for the incumbent to go round to private houses for baptisms, sometimes to baptise several infants in one house. He made his records on slips of paper, which may not have been copied into the register – such slips have been found at the bottom of the parish chest. Entries in the register, moreover, were often made weekly, and it was not difficult to forget to make one, as anybody knows who tries to make up his diary two or three days late. Sometimes the parish clerk kept the entries in a notebook, and entries have been found in such a book which are not in the official register.

Parish registers are not necessarily conclusive evidence that an infant grew up to be an adult, as burials are sometimes missing. This may, perhaps, explain some of the cases of unusual longevity. A son John is baptised, say in 1700, and dies in the same year, the burial record being omitted. Ten or even 20 years later another son is baptised with the same name (quite common, and in early days not unusual even when the first was still alive) and survives. His burial appearing in, say, 1780, may be related to the first baptism in error. It may be that only a will, naming sons in order of seniority, brings the error to light.

It must not be forgotten that sometimes the first child was baptised (and even buried when dying in infancy) in the mother's parish. A bride dying young may also be found buried in the parish of her childhood.

In the parish register will sometimes be found more than the bare records of names. The parish of a stranger, a description such as 'widow', a man's trade, given perhaps to distinguish two of the same name, all provide valuable evidence. A list of pew-holders is quite common and may sometimes be useful as evidence that a particular man was still in the parish at its date. A record of 'briefs' sometimes found may serve a similar purpose. These 'briefs' were a royal direction for contributions to some specific worthy object and have been described as 'almost an early equivalent of the Mansion House Fund or "this week's good cause"' (*The Parish Chest*, Tate). The contributions received were sometimes entered in full detail in the registers. A variety of other records and notes will be found, mostly of historical rather than genealogical interest.

Spelling will be found to be very erratic in the registers. Entries were often made by the parish clerk who spelt more or less phonetically: perhaps, too, he was sometimes a little deaf! One must remember that education (if reading and writing may be called education) is a product of a later age, and that in the 17th and 18th centuries there were comparatively few in a village who could read and write. On reference to the register entries on plate 3 (see pp.28-9), such words as Willam, Robord, Marey will be seen. If there are such mistakes in spelling with common Christian names, it is not surprising that surnames get distorted. For instance, 'Lafenton' on that page should, judging from baptism records elsewhere in the register, probably be 'Lavington'. It was, however, not ignorance only that was responsible; spelling, up to about the end of the 18th century, just did not matter. All varieties of a surname must therefore be taken together, though they should in each case be copied in the exact spelling found. For instance, the surname Willis has been found as Willes, Wyllys, Willys, Wilis, Willowes, Willice or Wilce, all obviously referring to the same name.

In reading parish registers one must remember the method of dating before the present-day calendar came into force in 1752. There used to be two methods of dating: one, that of the Church and the legal world, began the year at the Feast of Annunciation (i.e. Lady Day, 25 March), the other, used for historical purposes, beginning on 1 January. Consequently, an entry in a parish register of say, 3 February 1723, would be February in historical year 1724, and in pedigrees and other present-day references should be described as 3 February 1723/4. As from 1 January 1752, the year began for all purposes on 1 January. Reference to an extract from a register reproduced on plate 3 (see p.28) will show where the changes in the year came. For instance, consecutive entries are dated December 1742 and January 1742/3.

Parish registers are probably the most important source of genealogical information and the first to be examined after the birth, marriage and death records and census returns have been disposed of. Sometimes, however, they are not conclusive by themselves. Confusion may arise where fathers of the same Christian name and surname had children baptised in the same parish and over a similar period. Baptisms in later years usually give the name of father and mother, so a 'John, son of John and Alice X' will be known to be of a different family from 'Peter, son of John and Mary X'. If, however, the mother's name is not given in the register, as is often the case with early entries, and they merely appear as 'John, son of John X' and 'Peter, son of John X' there is nothing to separate the families. Here comes the value of wills, though, as will be seen in Chapter 8, the making of wills was not so common in the past as it is today.

A grandfather's will may refer to his son John and his children Peter, James and Henry, whereas another may refer to son John and his children, John, George and Alice. Baptisms of all will quite possibly have appeared in the same register but the wills sort out the families. The will, of course, need not necessarily be the grandfather's; it might be that of any relation.

Where registers are missing or gaps appear, enquiry should be made as to the existence of the Bishops' Transcripts referred to above. Although the Bishops' Transcripts are archives of the Diocesan Registry, in most dioceses they will be found deposited elsewhere. They may be at the County Record Office; if not, the County Archivist will be able to confirm where they are. The transcripts may be in bundles by years rather than arranged by parishes; if so, a good deal of time may be needed to search one particular parish over a number of years. A useful guide is J. Gibson's *Bishops' Transcripts and Marriage Licences, Bonds and Allegations* (5th ed. 2001) which covers the whole country; it gives the location and starting dates of the transcripts, which varies from one diocese to another. Transcripts of some registers of consular offices and Anglican chaplaincies abroad were sent to the London diocese and are now in Guildhall Library, London, who publish a list.

Even if the parish registers have been seen, it is as well to see the bishops' transcript, if available, when some expected entry cannot be found. Entries have been discovered in the transcripts which do not appear in the registers, which seems to indicate that the parson sometimes kept a rough list or book and did not enter up the register till after he had sent in the transcript.

The parish registers are, of course, those of the established Church of England. Though Nonconformists (or Dissenters) were not regular members of the established Church, they still, in their earlier days at any rate, were often baptised, married or buried there; indeed, following Lord Hardwicke's Marriage Act of 1754 everyone except Quakers and Jews had to be married in an Anglican church, a law which remained in force until 1837.

At the beginning of civil registration in 1837 nonconformist bodies were asked to send their registers to the Registrar General, and these are now available on microfilm at the Family Records Centre (see p.15). A list of them has been published (*List of Non-Parochial Registers in the Custody of the Registrar General*, H.M.S.O. 1859) and may be seen there, or will be found in some of the principal libraries. It will be seen that, generally speaking, the Roman Catholic and Jewish denominations did not do this, and their records must be looked for elsewhere. Moreover, there was no doubt neglect by others of the request, so that there is no guarantee that there are none extant in other places.

The Catholic Record Society has published certain Roman Catholic registers and the Huguenot Society of London some of those of French Protestants in this country. Some useful books have been written on both Huguenot and Jewish genealogy (see the Bibliography, p.108). If no record can be found from any of the above sources, inquiry should be made from the present authority of the denomination in the locality concerned as to whether any old records survive in their custody. The Society of Friends (Quakers) have their own central repository of records at Friends' House, Euston Road, London NW1 2BJ, telephone: 020 7663 1135, www.quaker.org.uk/library, which should be visited by anybody following ancestors of that persuasion. Though their registers should be with the non-parochial registers at the P.R.O., the Society made copies before surrendering them.

When the possibilities of parish registers have been exhausted, the most valuable source of information will be the record of wills and administrations. But, while the opportunity is there, examination should be made of other parish documents which will be found kept with the registers or otherwise in the charge of the incumbent. Something will be said of the value of these in the next chapter before dealing with the subject of wills.

Chapter 7
Other Parish Records

The majority of surviving parish records, other than the registers, are either concerned with the administration of Church funds or with the responsibility of the parish to the poor.

The general expense accounts of churchwardens are not likely to help much with the proof of a pedigree, but they often mention names of those to whom payment is made, and some information may be gathered of their status accordingly.

The records of rates levied are more useful. From quite early times the parishioners assembled as a 'vestry' had the power to levy a church rate for maintenance of the church fabric or other such purpose; later they were also responsible for making a rate to support the poor. The rate books of the parish, where surviving, will be found to record the names of parishioners and their assessments, so providing, like the lists of seatholders sometimes found in the registers, useful evidence of who was in the parish at the time and giving some idea of their substance.

However, perhaps the most valuable parish records for the genealogist, after the registers, are the 'settlement certificates' (see plate 4), sometimes found amongst parish papers, because by them can be proved the removal of a family, often otherwise very difficult to trace. These certificates were a result of the increasing burden of the poor on a parish. An Act of 1601 laid down that overseers were to be appointed to act with the

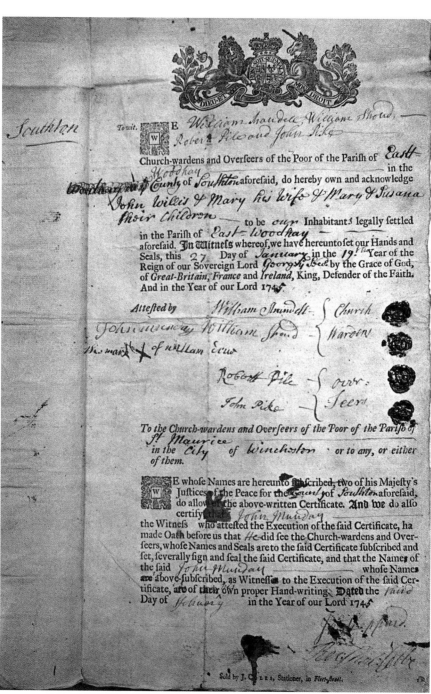

Plate 4 A Settlement Certificate
(from the Parish Records of St Maurice, Winchester)
(Reproduced by courtesy of the Hampshire Record Office)

churchwardens in maintaining the poor and providing them with work, and in 1662 another Act gave authority for removal of a stranger to his own parish unless he rented a property of the value of £10. It was by an Act of 1697 that the system of settlement certificates was established. A poor man was very restricted in his movements and was liable to be sent back to his own parish to be maintained there, if the necessity arose. He could acquire a settlement in a new parish under certain conditions, but, if he looked like being a charge on the parish, the authorities naturally did all they could to prevent a settlement. They had power to require him to obtain from his own parish a certificate that he was settled there, such certificate giving an undertaking to receive him back. These certificates were carefully kept as the authority for returning a man, and by that chance it has become sometimes easier to trace the movements of a poor family than those of the more prosperous classes. With the certificates may sometimes be found records of the declaration of their circumstances which these men had to make and such records often give information of family descent (see *Winchester Settlement Papers, 1667-1842*, Arthur J. Willis, 1967). Removal orders arising from the settlement certificates are also sometimes found.

Since the churchwardens and overseers were responsible for putting the poor to work they were often parties to apprenticeship deeds. They were empowered to place apprentices with the consent of the justices, and indentures may be found with the parish documents, again throwing light on the movement of the poorer members of the community. In some cases a borough would undertake the placing of apprentice (see *A Calendar of Southampton Apprenticeship Registers, 1609-1740*, Arthur J. Willis and A.L. Merson, Southampton Records Series, 1968).

Records of marriage licences (see p.62) may sometimes be found, particularly where the incumbent was a surrogate for granting licences. Their value is obvious. Tithe maps are parish records but copies are now in The National Archives and in the various county record offices. For further details see p.101.

A great variety of other documents may be found, from incumbents' diaries to certificates for touching for the King's evil (i.e., a certificate from the minister and churchwardens that a sufferer from scrofula had not before received the Royal touch which was supposed to cure it). When the parish of the family whose genealogy is being traced has been ascertained, all documents formerly in the parish chest or vestry cupboard should be examined for possible evidence. This may mean spending a long time, as there are not likely to be indexes, but it is a 'must'. In most cases all such documents will now be in the county record office, so enquiry should be made there first.

Chapter 8
Wills and Administrations

Before 1858 wills were a matter for ecclesiastical authority. Early wills will be found nearly always opening with a prayer for the testator's soul, committal of his body to the churchyard of his parish, sometimes followed by a legacy to the Church, before attention is turned to secular matters. The will was proved in the court of the archdeacon or bishop within whose archdeaconry or diocese respectively the property was held, except where some incumbent or other authority had 'peculiar' jurisdiction excluding these courts. Where property was held in more than one archdeaconry of a diocese the will had to be proved in the bishop's court, if in more than one diocese in the Prerogative Court of the Province – i.e., Canterbury or York. The exact rules deciding which was the proper court in which to prove a will are now rather obscure, as there were periods during a 'visitation' when one minor court was 'inhibited' and recourse must be had to a superior authority. The above general rule will, however, give a guide as to where to look first. If a particular will is not found where it may be expected, the possibility of a superior court should be examined. During the Commonwealth from about 1652 to 1660 ecclesiastical jurisdiction in the matter of wills was suspended and all wills had to be proved before a civil authority in London. On the Restoration jurisdiction was restored to the Church.

By the Court of Probate Act of 1857 the Principal Probate Registry was established in London with a number of District Registries subordinated to it, and the Church was finally

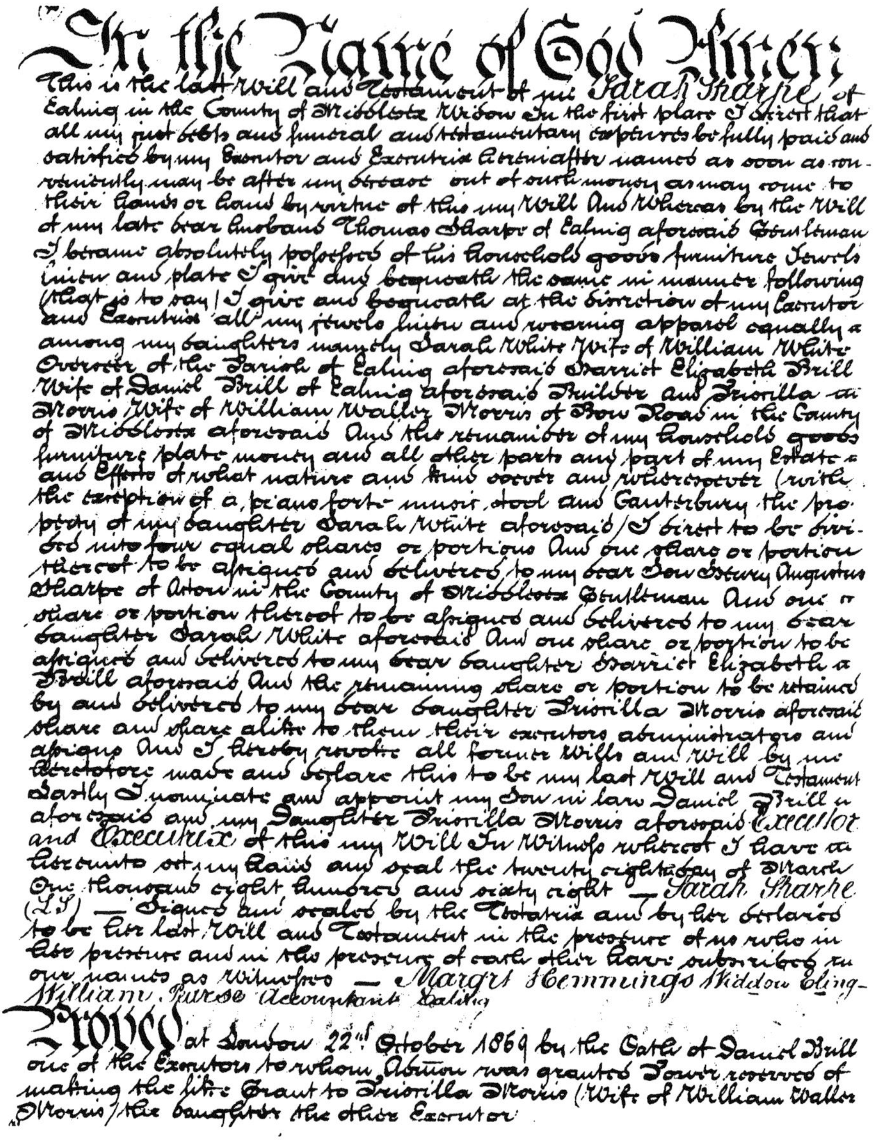

In the Name of God Amen

This is the last Will and Testament of me Sarah Sharpe of Ealing in the County of Middlesex Widow In the first place I direct that all my just debts and funeral and testamentary expenses be fully paid and satisfied by my Executor and Executrix hereinafter named as soon as conveniently may be after my decease out of such money as may come to their hands or hand by virtue of this my Will And Whereas by the Will of my late dear husband Thomas Sharpe of Ealing aforesaid Gentleman I became absolutely possessed of his household goods furniture jewels linen and plate I give and bequeath the same in manner following (that is to say) I give and bequeath at the direction of my Executor and Executrix all my jewels linen and wearing apparel equally among my daughters namely Sarah White Wife of William White Overseer of the Parish of Ealing aforesaid Harriet Elizabeth Brill Wife of Daniel Brill of Ealing aforesaid Builder and Priscilla Morris Wife of William Walter Morris of Bow Road in the County of Middlesex aforesaid And the remainder of my household goods furniture plate money and all other parts and part of my Estate and Effects of what nature and kind soever and wheresoever (with the exception of a pianoforte music stool and Canterbury the property of my daughter Sarah White aforesaid) I direct to be divided into four equal shares or portions And one share or portion thereof to be assigned and delivered to my dear Henry Augustus Sharpe of Acton in the County of Middlesex Gentleman And one or share or portion thereof to be assigned and delivered to my dear daughter Sarah White aforesaid And one share or portion to be assigned and delivered to my dear daughter Harriet Elizabeth a Brill aforesaid And the remaining share or portion to be retained by and delivered to my dear daughter Priscilla Morris aforesaid share and share alike to them their executors administrators and assigns And I hereby revoke all former Wills and Will by me heretofore made and declare this to be my last Will and Testament Lastly I nominate and appoint my son in law Daniel Brill aforesaid and my daughter Priscilla Morris aforesaid Executor and Executrix of this my Will In Witness whereof I have to account set my hand and seal the twenty eighth day of March One thousand eight hundred and sixty eight — Sarah Sharpe (LS) — Signed and sealed by the Testatrix and by her declared to be her last Will and Testament in the presence of us who in her presence and in the presence of each other have subscribed our names as witnesses — Margrt Hemmings Widow Ealing William Purse Accountant Ealing

Proved at London 22nd October 1869 by the oath of Daniel Brill one of the Executors to whom Admon was granted Power reserved of making the like Grant to Priscilla Morris (Wife of William Walter Morris) the daughter the other Executor

Plate 5 A 19th-century Will
(from the Principal Registry of the Family Division)

TRANSCRIPT OF PLATE 5

In the Name of God Amen This is the last Will and Testament of me *Sarah Sharpe* of Ealing in the County of Middlesex Widow. In the first place I direct that all my just debts and funeral and testamentary expenses be fully paid and satisfied by my Executor and Executrix hereinafter named as soon as conveniently may be after my decease, out of such money as may come to their hands or hand by virtue of this my Will. And Whereas by the Will of my late husband Thomas Sharpe of Ealing aforesaid Gentleman I became absolutely possessed of his household goods, furniture, Jewels, linen and plate, I give and bequeath at the discretion of my Executor and Executrix all my jewels, linen and wearing apparel equally among my daughters namely Sarah White Wife of William White, Overseer of the Parish of Ealing aforesaid, Harriet Elizabeth Brill Wife of Daniel Brill of Ealing aforesaid, Builder, and Priscilla Morris Wife of William Waller Morris of Bow Road in the County of Middlesex aforesaid. And the remainder of my household goods, furniture, plate, money and all other parts and part of my Estate and Effects of what nature and kind soever and wheresoever (with the exception of a pianoforte music stool and Canterbury, the property of my daughter Sarah White aforesaid), I direct to be divided into four equal shares or portions, And one share or portion thereof to be assigned and delivered to my dear Son Henry Augustus Sharpe of Acton in the County of Middlesex Gentleman, And one share or portion thereof to be assigned and delivered to my dear daughter Sarah White aforesaid, And one share or portion to be assigned and delivered to my dear daughter Harriet Elizabeth Brill aforesaid, And the remaining share or portion to be retained by and delivered to my dear daughter Priscilla Morris aforesaid, share and share alike, to them, their executors, administrators and assigns. And I hereby revoke all former Wills and Will by me heretofore made and declare this to be my last Will and Testament. Lastly I nominate and appoint my Son in law Daniel Brill aforesaid and my Daughter Priscilla Morris aforesaid *Executor and Executrix* of this my Will. In Witness whereof I have hereunto set my hand and seal the twenty eighth day of March One thousand eight hundred and sixty eight – *Sarah Sharpe (LS)* – Signed and sealed by the Testatrix and by her declared to be her last Will and Testament in the presence of us who in her presence and in the presence of each other have subscribed our names as Witnesses – *Margrt Hemmings Widdow Eling* [sic] – *William Pearse Accountant Ealing.*

Proved at London 22nd October 1869 by the Oath of Daniel Brill one of the Executors to whom Admon [Administration] was granted, Power reserved of making the like Grant to Priscilla Morris (Wife of William Waller Morris) the daughter, the other Executor.

Note: Some punctuation has been added for the sake of clarity.

deprived of the jurisdiction. The wills and other records of the ecclesiastical probate courts were handed over to other authorities, and are now in the care of local county record offices or libraries. The records of the Prerogative Court of Canterbury (including wills proved during the Commonwealth period, as mentioned above) can be seen on microfilm at the Family Records Centre, 1 Myddelton Street, London EC1R 1UW, telephone 020 8392 5300, www.familyrecords.gov.uk/frc (opening times given in Chapter 4, p.15); further details below (p.51). Those of the Prerogative Court of York are at the Borthwick Institute of Historical Research, St Anthony's Hall, Peaseholme Green, York YO1 7PW, telephone: 01904 642315, www. york.ac.uk/inst/bihr.

In such Church records will be found original wills (or copies) filed according to date of probate. In some cases 'Probate Act Books' may be available in which are entered all the probates granted. For some periods, too, there may be volumes of 'registered copies', i.e., volumes in which the wills have been transcribed in full as each was proved, often with the probate act following it. Practically the whole period for which wills are extant in the Prerogative courts is covered by such registered copies bound up in large volumes.

Where there was no will or some irregularity in it, letters of administration, commonly abbreviated to 'admons.', were granted, as they are today. The bonds entered into by the administrators may be found available in some cases and, just as for probates, there may be an (Admon.) Act Book. Administration may be granted with the will annexed, if, for example, no executor is named or the executor has renounced or died before completing distribution of the estate.

With both proved wills and admons. it will often be found, particularly in the earlier cases, that an inventory is filed with the papers; sometimes an inventory may be there and the will missing, but the admon. may be endorsed on the inventory. The gaps in wills are many, but one must remember that in the 16th and 17th centuries there was not the necessity for a will that there is now.

Many were tenants of a manor, so had no real estate to dispose of and there were none of the registered securities that there are today, which need proof of title before a transfer can be made. Property was mostly portable and no doubt the family divided the farm stock, furniture, etc., according to the known wishes of the deceased or by mutual agreement between themselves. In early days there was little means of investment for cash, except perhaps money lent on a bond, so pecuniary legacies were few.

There are printed indexes to many of the wills proved in the pre-1858 probate courts, and others have MS or typescript indexes, in bound volumes or card indexes (often now available on microfilm or fiche). Nearly all of these can be seen on microfilm at the Society of Genealogists' Library. An essential guide through the maze of overlapping probate courts is *Probate jurisdictions: where to look for wills* by J. Gibson and E. Churchill (5th ed. 2002). This is arranged by county and within each county by the various probate courts and record repositories, with details of the present location of wills, period of coverage and existence of indexes.

Having studied this guide to find out which was the court having jurisdiction in the locality concerned, one will have to visit the appropriate repository which will have an index of names and produce the documents. In some cases there will be published or online lists which can be examined beforehand. It should not be forgotten that if a will cannot be found there may be an admon. (usually listed separately) which may give some information on next of kin.

It is advisable to know the date and place of death of the testator whose will is being searched for. If the place is known the will should be looked for in the indexes of the bishop's court of the diocese, and the relative archdeacon's court or, if it

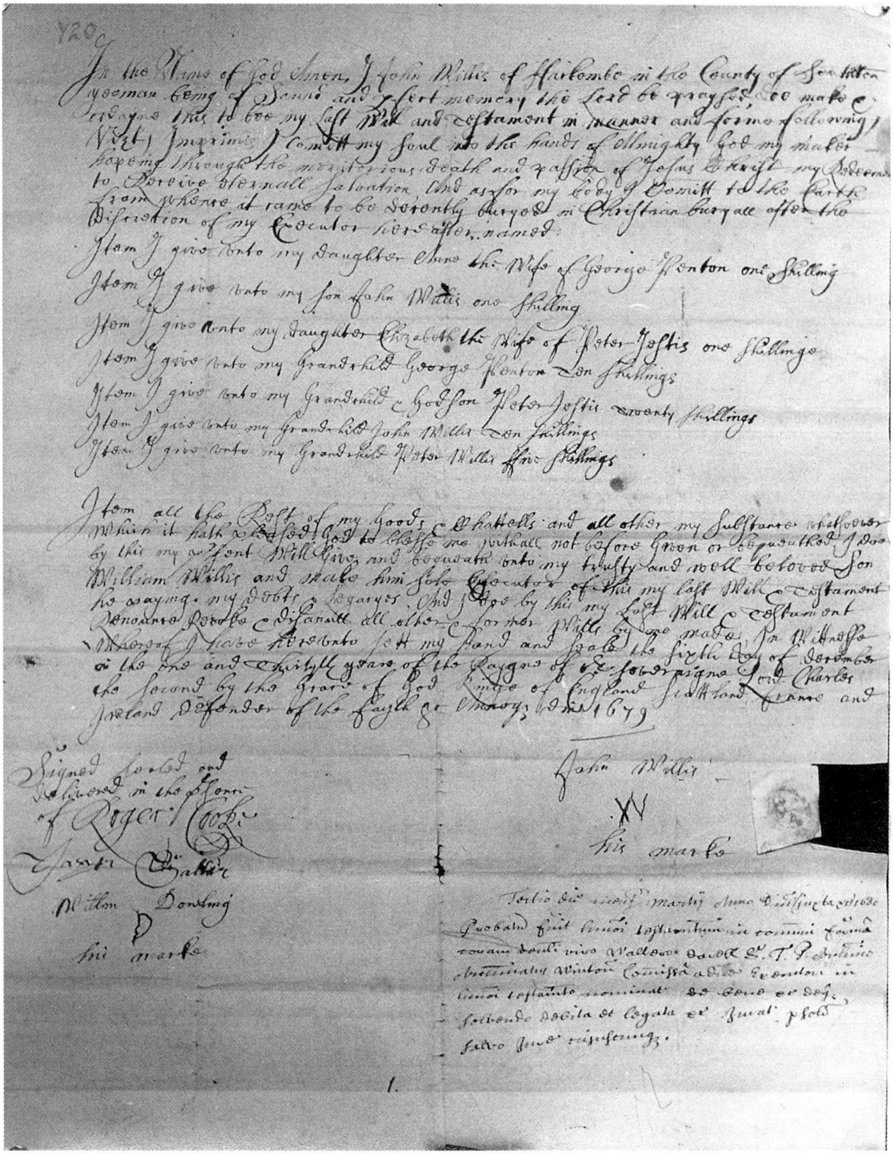

Plate 6 A 17th-century Will
(from the District Probate Registry, Winchester, Archdeacon's Court 1860)
(Reproduced by courtesy of the Hampshire Record Office)

TRANSCRIPT OF PLATE 6

In the Name of God Amen, I John Willis of Fackombe in the County of Southampton, yeoman, being of sound and perfect memory the Lord be praysed, doe make and ordayne this to be my last Will and Testament in manner and forme following vizt.: Imprimis 1 committ my soul into the hands of Almightly God my maker hopeing through the meritorious death and passion of Jesus Christ my Redeemer to receive eternal Salvation. And as for my body 1 committ to the Earth from whence it came to be decently buryed in Christian buryall after the discretion of my Executor hereafter named

   Item I give unto my daughter Anne the wife of George Penton one shilling
   Item I give unto my son John Willis one shilling
   Item I give unto my daughter Elizabeth the wife of Peter Jestis one shillinge
   Item I give unto my grandchild George Penton ten shillings
   Item I give unto my grandchild and godson Peter Jestis twenty shillings
   Item I give unto my grandchild John Willis ten shillings
   Item I give unto my grandchild Peter Willis five shillings
   Item all the rest of my goods and chattels and all other my substance whatsoever which it hath pleased God to blesse me withall not before given or bequeathed 1 doe by this my present Will give and bequeath unto my trusty and well beloved son William Willis and make him sole executor of this my last Will and Testament he paying my debts and legacies. And I do by this my last Will and Testament renounce revoke and disannull all other and former wills by me made. In Witnesse whereof I have hereunto sett my hand and seale the sixth day of December in the one and thiryeth yeare of the raygne of the Sovereign Lord Charles the Second by the Grace of God Kinge of England Scottland france and Ireland defender of the fayth etc. annoque domini 1679

	John Willis
Signed sealed and	W
delivered in the	his marke
psence of	tertio die mens. Martii anno Dni (juxta &c.*)
	1680 probatum fuit hmoi. (hujusmodi)
Roger Cooke	testamentum. in communi forma coram venli.
Jasper Salter	(venerabili) viro Waltero Darrell S.T.P. (Sacrae
William Dowling	Theologiae Professori) Archino (Archidiacono)
D	Archinatus Winton. Commissa adm(inistratio)
his marke	executori in hmoi. testamento nominat(o) de
	bene etc. denique solvendo debita et legata etc.
	Jurato personaliter salvo Jure cuiuscunque.†

   * Elsewhere found to represent 'juxta cursum et computacionem Ecclesie Anglicane'.
   † On the third day of the month of March in the year of Our Lord 1680/1 the said will was proved in common form in the presence of the Venerable Walter Darell, D.D., Archdeacon of Winchester. Administration was granted to the executor named in the said will, he having personally sworn to administer justly and pay the debts and legacies etc. without prejudice to the rights of any other person.

appears from the list of 'Peculiars' in the diocese that one of these may have had jurisdiction, the index of Peculiar Courts should be examined. Failing these, the Prerogative Court list of the province should be searched, where the will would have been proved if the testator owned property in more than one diocese. Wills proved during the Commonwealth whilst the authority of the ecclesiastical courts was suspended will be found with P.C.C. wills.

In 1858 the Court of Probate was established, and all wills and admons. are now held by the Principal Registry of the Family Division, whose indexes can be searched at the Probate Department, First Avenue House, 42-49 High Holborn, London WC1V 6NP, telephone: 020 7947 6000, www.courtservice.gov.uk (click on 'Using the Courts'). The opening hours are Monday-Friday, 10.00 am-4.30 pm. Searching the indexes is free, but there is a charge, currently £5, for a copy of a will and probate grant, which in some cases can be done immediately, but is usually sent by post; there is little point in paying for a copy of a grant of administration, as the full details are given in the index volumes. The indexes are printed and arranged alphabetically for each year, so it is helpful to have an approximate idea of the date of death (always remembering that a will could have been proved in the year after the death, so it is worth searching on for a year or two if the entry does not turn up in the expected year).

In the case of a common surname the searcher should be able to identify the particular will by the Christian name, place of death and other details given in the indexes.

Copies of the indexes are available on microfiche (1858-1943 only) at the Family Records Centre, and also in some major public libraries and District Probate Registries; there are copies on microfilm at the Society of Genealogists, covering the years 1858-1930. From the information given in these, copies of wills can be ordered, by post only, from The Postal Searches & Copies Dept., York Probate Sub-Registry, Castle Chambers,

Clifford Street, York YO1 9RG, telephone: 01904 666777; the charge is currently £5, and this same fee will also cover a search for four years from the date of death if you would like the staff to make the search for you.

Something further should also be said about the P.C.C. wills at The National Archives (P.R.O.). These can be seen on microfilm at the Family Records Centre, 1 Myddelton Street, London EC1R 1UW (see p.15 for current opening hours), as well as at Kew (see p.70).

There are printed indexes for the years 1383-1700, and also for 1750-1800, and 1853-57, and a new index on microfiche for 1701-49, but for the remaining years it will be necessary to consult the MS indexes (PROB 12) in the search room. These are arranged by year, but are not fully alphabetical, with surnames grouped together by their initial letter. Once the required will has been found, the year of probate and the folio number should be noted. The class list volume (PROB 11) will then provide the reference number for the relevant volume of wills: for instance, a will proved in 1587, folio 34, would be found in the volume PROB 11/70 (which includes folio numbers 1-40). The microfilm for the correct volume can then be located and taken to the microfilm reader.

At this point it will be found that there are two sets of numbers on the pages of wills – stamped numbers on every right-hand page, and a handwritten number (Roman numerals in the early volumes) at the top right-hand corner of every 16 pages. This is the folio number referred to in the indexes, and the will required is to be found in the 16 pages following that number, marked by the testator's name in the margin.

P.C.C. Administrations are to be found in a separate series under the reference PROB 6, or PROB 7 for 'special' or 'limited' grants of administration from 1810 onwards only. Inventories survive for some wills, mainly for the period 1666-1730, and there are separate class lists for them.

An Inventory of all & singuler of the goods Chattle & Catell
of John Millet the elder late of Gatcombe in the County of
Southton died & seazed of vallued & apprized the 28th
day of february Anno dom 1680 by for whose names
are herevnto subscribed

Inprimis all his wearing Apparell & money in purse
in the Chamber where he died ——————— 2 — 0 — 0

Item one feather bedd & bedsteed & all
that thereunto belongeth ————————— 2 — 0 — 0

Item one Coffer one Chaire ——————————— 0 — 4 — 0

Item certaine Cheese ——————————————— 0 — 10 — 0

Item in the Chamber over the hall
one flock bed one bedsteed with all there
vnto belonging ————————————————— 0 — 10 — 0

It in the hall one payre of Andirons
three Cottrells one speet one fireshovell
& tonges ————————————————————— 0 — 8 — 0

Item one brass pott one brass Kettle
allso one brass Candlestick & fowre
pewter dishes one lanterne ——————————— 0 — 6 — 0

Item one Joyned Cubbord one forme
and two Chaires ————————————————— 0 — 6 — 0

Item fowre flitches of bacon ————————— 2 — 0 — 0

Item one salt hier in the outhouse
allso one Cheese press & kett racket ———— 1 — 0 — 0

Item in the drinke house two barrills
one stand one table bord ——————————— 0 — 10 — 0

Item in the stable two horses &
the harness belonging to them ——————— 6 — 0 — 0

Item in the backside three Cowes &
three yearling bullocks ——————————— 10 — 0 — 0

allso two store pigs

Ite one Carte ——————————————————— 0 — 14 — 0

Item fower score sheep ———————————— 3 — 0 — 0

Item in the barnet certaine wheat ————— 24 — 0 — 0

early oates pease throshed & vnthroshed ——— 15 — 13 — 4

Item Corne vpon the ground beinge
by estimation eight acres of wheat & oatshet — 8 — 0 — 0

Robert Saker
Thomas Golfe appryzers

Sume total ———— 78 — 1 — 4

TRANSCRIPT OF PLATE 7

An inventory of all and singuler the goods chatle and catell late of John Willis the elder late of Fackcombe in the County of Southampton died seazed of vallued and apprized the 28th day of Feberuary anno domi 1680 by us whose names are hereunto subscribed.

	li	s	d
Imprimis all his wearing Apparill and money in purse in the Chamber where he died	2	0	0
Item one feather beed & bedsteed & all that thereunto, belongeth	2	0	0
Item one Coffer one Chaire		4	0
Item certaine Cheese		10	0
Item in the Chamber over the hall one Flocke beed & bedsteed with all thereunto belonging		10	0
Item in the hall one peere [pair] of Andiornes [andirons] three Cottrills one speet one fireshoovell & tonges		8	0
Item one brase pott one brase Keetle allso	1	0	0
one brase Candlesticke & foure peuter dishes one lanterne	6	0	
Item one Joyend Cubord one Forme and two Chaires	6	0	
Item foure fliches of baccon	2	0	0
Item one salt kiver in the outhouse allso one Cheese preese and billet hatchets	1	0	0
Item in the drinke house two barrils one stand one Table bord	1	0	0
Item in the Stable two horses and the harness belonging to them	6	0	0
Item in the backside three Cowes and three yearling bullocks	10	0	0
allso two store pigs		14	0
Item one Carte	3	0	0
Item Fouer score sheep	24	0	0
Item in the barnes certaine wheat barly oats & pease threshed and unthreshed	15	13	4
Item Corne upon the ground being by estimation eight acres of wheat & vetches	8	0	0
Sum total	78	1	4

(sgd) Robert Lake   Appreisers
       Thomas Self

Photocopies from the microfilms can easily be produced on the spot for a small charge, or the staff will do this for you if you prefer.

P.C.C. Wills from 1670-1858 can also be searched online by name, place and occupation, at The National Archives' Documents Online website (www.documentsonline.pro.gov.uk); the images have been digitised and can be downloaded for a fee of £3.

There is one other important category of probate records at The National Archives (P.R.O.), also available on microfilm at the Family Records Centre. These are the Death Duty Registers, starting in 1796, when duty became payable on estates over a certain value. As this applied to only a small percentage of estates until 1815, not many wills are to be found in these records until after that date, but for the years 1815-58 the index volumes (IR 27) can be a useful way of tracking down a will without having to search the individual indexes to several different probate courts. The registers, with details of the estate and beneficiaries, are under the reference IR 26, and are an invaluable substitute for the original wills for the counties of Somerset and Devon, whose probate records were destroyed in the bombing of Exeter in 1942.

As with parish registers, some difficulty may be experienced in actually reading the will, when it has been tracked down, and this applies as much to the register copies as to the original wills. Indeed, the formal legal hand used for the 18th- and 19th-century registers of P.C.C. and later wills is often harder to decipher than the handwriting of the 17th century. An example, with transcript, is shown in Plate 5 (p.44). The booklets referred to in Chapter 6 (see p.33) will be found equally useful for reading wills, and there is a great advantage in obtaining a photocopy, so that the document can be studied at leisure and in comfort, without the embarrassment of having to admit to being unable to make head or tail of it. Even so, there will always be bad handwriting, just as there is today, and in many cases documents have become worn or damaged over the years, so some wills would tax the skill of even an experienced record searcher. Another problem, usually first encountered with probate records, is the use of Latin, which was commonly used for grants of probate and administration until the 18th century. However, before despair sets in, bear in mind that there is no need to have studied the language at school, as probate grants are of a standard form, and once the basic layout has become familiar it is fairly easy to pick out the relevant details of name, place and date. A grant begins with the word 'Probatum', not used for administrations, but in both cases the grant is expressed as 'admio. [administratio] commissa fuit ...' followed by the name(s) of the grantee, and their relationship. The sort of words which occur at this point are 'filio', 'fratri', 'sorori', 'patri' (son, brother, sister, father), or the more complicated 'nepoti ex filia' (a grandson by the daughter, i.e. a grandson who is a daughter's son) or 'nepoti ex fratre' (a nephew, son of a brother).

The date is usually written in words, so a knowledge of the Latin words for numerals is valuable, but the year may be in Arabic numerals. In early records the year may be expressed in Roman numerals, but these can be copied down and worked out later on, rather than risk a miscalculation which then throws a whole pedigree into confusion. It should be noted that the last 'i' in Roman figures is written as a 'j', thus viij = 8.

The date, when between 1 January and 24 March (before 1752, see p.35) may be followed by 'juxta &c,' or 'stylo Angl.' These phrases mean that the year was reckoned as beginning on 25 March, and consequently such a reference after (for example) 20 January 1720 would mean 1720/21, 1721 being the modern dating.

There is a useful copy of a grant of administration, with translation, in *Tracing Your Ancestors in the Public Record Office* by A. Bevan (2002). Other handbooks to help with the Latin are

Basic Approach to Latin for Family Historians by M. Gandy (1995) and the larger but more comprehensive *Latin for Local and Family Historians* by D. Stuart (1995). The amount of information obtainable from wills varies considerably. In some of the more ancient ones the testator sometimes aggravatingly refers to relationships without giving names, or to 'kinsmen' without giving relationship. He may leave everything to one person or make the genealogist rub his hands with glee by mentioning all the members of a large family including 'his sisters, his cousins and his aunts'. One would naturally search first for the family name but almost equally important may be the wills of 'in laws' – a father-in-law or mother-in-law (being a widow), may well leave property to the family and particularly mention grandchildren (bear in mind that 'father-in-law' may mean 'step-father'). Uncles and aunts, too, may mention their nephews and nieces, great-nephews and great-nieces. The names of families allied by marriage should be noted for this purpose.

In the will on p.48 Ann Penton and Elizabeth Jestis are daughters and their children named George and Peter respectively are entered in the pedigree (see pp.116-22). Their line is not pursued as they have left the Willis family and name.

One must not forget that until the Married Women's Property Act of 1882 the property of a married woman was with some exceptions, such as property held under a settlement, that of her husband, and that, therefore, if she predeceased her husband she could normally leave no will. Once she was widowed, she could, of course, dispose of property.

When a required will has been found, an abstract of it should be made on a separate sheet for filing as suggested in Chapter 2. The following information should always be noted:

Record office or other repository where the will was seen, whether it was the original or a copy, and the repository's reference number

Name of testator

Occupation and/or address (in old wills probably only the parish), if given

Date when the will was made

Place of burial desired (this may indicate a family move)

Names and relationship of all beneficiaries

Particulars of all landed estate mentioned

Names of executors, supervisors and overseers (if any)

Names of witnesses

Particulars of heraldic seal (if any)

Date and place of probate, and to whom granted

In individual cases there may be some special mention which should be recorded. For instance, the articles bequeathed may be of family interest though not material evidence genealogically. It may be mentioned that it is common in a will to see a legacy of one shilling (see plate 6, p.49). This is not an example of the popular phrase 'cut him off with a shilling'. It is usually included to indicate that the individual is not forgotten, where he has had his portion, perhaps, in the testator's lifetime.

Nor must it be assumed where administration is granted to a creditor, the widow renouncing, that the testator was necessarily bankrupt. It may be merely a means of preventing a rush of small creditors who would eat up the estate.

It must not be forgotten that a will reflects conditions at the time it was written, not at the time of death. If some years have elapsed, children born in the interval will not be mentioned by name (though the possibility of their birth may be provided for in anticipation). Legatees, too, or others mentioned in the will may have predeceased the testator.

When the possibilities of parish records, census returns and wills – the leading sources – have been exhausted, one must consider the great variety of other sources which might help, and decide which is the most likely. Firstly, there are other classes of ecclesiastical records which give genealogical information, and should be considered next, before turning to national and local records in The National Archives and other libraries and record offices.

The relevance of the various sources suggested will, of course, depend on the occupation and status of the family concerned, so, before plunging in, it is worth deciding which is the most likely to be of use.

Chapter 9

Other Ecclesiastical Records

The subject of parish registers and the bishops' transcripts, the best known of ecclesiastical records, has already been discussed in Chapter 6, as one can hardly touch genealogy without them. Other parochial records have been mentioned in Chapter 7. But there are a number of other sources of genealogical value amongst what might be called regional ecclesiastical archives.

The hierarchy of the established Church of England now consists of the two archbishops, the diocesan bishops with assistant or suffragan bishops, archdeacons, rural deans and parochial clergy. Except for rural deans, who do not seem to have any ancient records, and the assistant and suffragan bishops, each of these categories has archives representing the work of their predecessors. The archives of diocesan bishops were in the charge of their diocesan registrar and those of archdeacons were with their 'Official', usually a solicitor having a relation to the archdeacon like that of the registrar to the bishop. In a different category is the dean or provost of a cathedral. He and the canons who form the chapter are responsible for the maintenance and services of the cathedral and are not part of the episcopal administrative authorities. The archives of the dean and chapter will normally be found in the cathedral library.

Noverint Universi per præsentes; Nos *John Willis de Hursley in Com Southton Pipemaker et Rogerum Bond de Hursley ... Pipemaker teneri & firmiter Obligari ... in Christo Patri ac dno dno Jonathan ... divina Winton Epo ...* in ——— libris bonæ & legalis Monetæ Magnæ Britaniæ, solvend' eidem ... —aut suo certo Attornato, Executoribus, Administratoribus, vel assignatis suis: Ad quam quidem solutionem bene & fideliter faciend' Obligamus Nos & utrumque nostrum per se pro toto & in solido, Hæredes, Executores, & Administratores nostros firmiter per præsentes. Sigillis nostris Sigillat' Dat' ... *dis mensis May Anno Regni Dni nri Georgii Dei gra Mag Brit Franciæ & Hiberniæ Regis Fidei Defensor & quarto Annoq; Dni 1718°*

THE Condition of this Obligation is such, That if there shall not hereafter appear any Lawful Lett or Impediment, by Reason of any Pre-contract, Consanguinity, Affinity, or any other just Cause whatsoever; but that *the above bounden John Willis a Batchelour and Mary Marchant of Hursley aforsd Spinster* ——

may lawfully Marry together; and that there is not any Suit depending before any Judge Ecclesiastical or Civil, for, or concerning any such Pre-contract: And that the Consent of the Parents, or others the Governours of the said Parties, be thereunto first had and obtain'd. And that they cause their said Marriage to be openly solemniz'd in the Face of the Parish Church of *St Thomas in the Citty of Winchester* —— between the Hours of Eight and Twelve of the Clock in the Forenoon: And do and shall save harmless, and keep Indemnified the above-nam'd *Lord Bishop his Chancelor and* —— his Surrogates, and all other his Officers, and Successors in Office, for and concerning the Premises; That then this Obligation to be void and of none effect, or else to remain in full force and vertue.

Signat' Sigillat' & Deliberat'
in præsentia.

Jehis Dawkins   *John Willis*
                   Roger Bond

Plate 8   A Marriage Licence Bond
(from the Records of the Diocesan Registrar, Winchester)
(Reproduced by courtesy of the Hampshire Record Office)

TRANSCRIPT OF LATIN PART OF PLATE 8

Noverint Universi per praesentes; Nos *Joh[ann]em Willis de Hursley in Com[itatu] South[amp]ton[ie] Pipemaker et Rogerum Pond de Hursley p[re]d[icto] Pipemaker teneri & firm[iter] obligari Rev[eren]do in Christo Patri ac D[omi]no D[omi]no*[sic] *Jonathani P[er]m[ission]e Divina Winton[ie] Ep[iscop]o* in *Centum* libris bonae & legalis Monetae Magnae Britanniae, solvend[is] eidem *Rev[eren]do P[a]tri* aut suo certo Attornato, Executoribus, Administratoribus, vel assignatis suis: Ad quam quidem solutionem bene & fideliter faciend[am] Obligamus Nos & utrumque nostrum per se pro toto & in solido, Haeredes, Executores, & Administratores nostros firmiter per praesentes. Sigillis nostris Sigillat[as] Dat[um] *Decimo Septimo die Mensis Maij Anno Regni D[omi[ni N[ost]ri Georgij Dei gra[tia] Mag[ne] Brit[annie] Francie & Hib[er]nie Regis Fidei Defensor[is] Etc quarto Annoque D[omi]ne 1718.*

TRANSLATION

Know all men by (these) presents that we *John Willis of Hursley in the county of Southampton Pipemaker and Roger Pond of Hursley aforesaid Pipemaker are held and firmly bound to the Reverend Father in Christ and Lord Jonathan by divine permission Bishop of Winchester,* in *one hundred* pounds of good and lawful money of Great Britain to be paid to the said Reverend Father or his certain attorney, executors, administrators or assigns: to making which payment indeed well and faithfully we bind ourselves and each of us by himself for the whole (sum) and for the whole (we bind) our heirs, executors and administrators firmly by (these) presents. Sealed with our seals given *the seventeenth day of May in the fourth year of the reign of our Lord George by the Grace of God King of Great Britain, France and Ireland, Defender of the Faith etc. and in the year of the Lord 1718.*

TRANSCRIPT OF HANDWRITING ONLY IN ENGLISH PART

.....the above bounden John Willis a Batchelour and Mary Marchant of Hursley afores[ai]d Spinster ......
.....St. Thomas in the Citty[sic] of Winchester......
.....Lord Bishop his Chancelor[sic] and......

In recent years there has been a tendency towards transfer of episcopal and archdeacons' ancient records from the official custodian who is busy with current work to such a repository as a county or municipal record office, where there is an expert staff for cataloguing and repair and proper storage accommodation, but some are still with diocesan registrars.

MARRIAGE LICENCES

One of the most valuable items for the genealogist is the set of marriage licence allegations. These are the documents on which the licences were issued and consist of an affidavit supported by a bond (the bond was discontinued in 1823-4). See plate 8, pp.60-1.

The affidavit is normally by one of the parties, often giving his trade or occupation, declaring that there is no lawful impediment by consanguinity or other cause. It may state the age of each party (valuable for tracing baptism records) or simply declare that they are over twenty-one. Where either of the parties is under 21, the consent of parent or guardian may be endorsed or be in a separate document, so giving valuable genealogical evidence. The affidavit will also state the church in which the marriage is to be solemnized, a pointer to the parish register for the entry.

The bond is given by two sureties, one normally being one of the parties. It vouches that there is no impediment to the marriage. The bondsman's name is sometimes useful, being that of perhaps a father or brother.

A large proportion of these marriage licence records has been printed and indexed, particularly by the Harleian Society and the British Record Society, and also by local societies and individuals. For further details on the location of original records and indexes, reference should be made to *Bishop's Transcripts and Marriage Licences, Bonds and Allegations: Guide to their Location and Indexes*, by J. Gibson (5th ed., 2001) which also details the dates for which these records survive in the different dioceses.

COURT PAPERS

The ecclesiastical courts, besides having jurisdiction over testamentary matters, heard many disputes about tithes, actions of defamation (slander), matrimonial disputes and sexual offences and various causes of a disciplinary nature arising from behaviour of churchwardens or other officials, disputes about seating, etc. Testamentary causes will, of course, quite often give information about relationships, but the others may not give much but biographical information, except for one important category.

As in the Court of Chancery, so in the ecclesiastical courts evidence was taken by deposition, and the deponent gave his place of birth, age, and previous places of residence. The value of these records to the genealogist will depend very largely on whether they have been indexed. It should be mentioned that (as with most evidence of age) one must use the age given with allowance made for a margin both ways. Ages sometimes seem to be given to the nearest five years, and, no doubt, there were occasions when the deponent did not know with any accuracy.

There was one thing which, though nominally a matter for the bishop's court, was probably largely administrative in character, viz. the appointment of guardians for minors. This mostly arose when a minor on the death of his parents wanted to prove a will, but was not able to do so because of his status. The court appointed somebody, usually a near relation, to act on his behalf. Two documents are found: the appointment of the guardian by name, signed and sealed by the minor (if under the age of seven, and so an 'infant', the deed was signed by a near relative on his behalf); and the Act of Court making the appointment signed by the vicar general or his surrogate. Sometimes several brothers and sisters are covered by the same deed. As the names and ages

Twentieth day of July one Thousand Seven
Hundred and Seventy Six

Know all Men by these Presents that I

Richard Whitmaich a Minor of the Age of ten Years or thereabouts one of
the natural and lawful Children and also eldest Son and Heir at Law
of Richard Whitmaich late of the Parish of Whippingham in the Isle of Wight
in the County of Southampton and (Diocese) of Winchester Yeoman died Have
made authorized appointed and chosen and by these Presents DO make, authorize
appoint and chose my beloved Mother Elizabeth Whitmaich Widow relict of my
said late Father Richard Whitmaich dead to be my true and lawful Guardian
or Curator to take care of and receive to and for my Use and Benefit
during my Minority all and every such Monies Rents and arrears of Rent if
any Issues and profits which I am by reason of the (Death of my said late
Father interested in or intitled to from by and out of the Rents Copyhold and
Personal Estate or Estates he was by Virtue of the last Will and Testament
of Richard Whitmaich late of Newport aforesaid Yeoman deed or otherwise
howsoever interested in or intitled unto And for me to give and execute any
Release or other proper (Discharges for the same And that this my Proxy
or nomination of Guardian or Curator may have due effect in Law I do
hereby impower and authorize Richard Holloway Notary Public one of the
Procurators General of the Consistory Court of the Lord Bishop of Winchester
to be my true and lawful Proctor for me and in my Name to appear before
the Worshipful George Harris Clerk Dr of Laws Vicar General and Official
Principal of the Right Reverend Father in God John by Divine permission
Lord Bishop of Winchester or his lawful Surrogate or any other competent
Judge in this Behalf and to exhibit this my Proxy and to pray and
procure the same to be admitted and enacted and generally to do all
other Acts and Things in this behalf necessary to be done and executed hereby
ratifying and confirming all and whatsoever my said Proctor shall
lawfully do or cause to be done in the Premises by Virtue of these presents
In Witness whereof I have hereunto set my Hand and Seal this
day and Year first above written.

Sealed and delivered (being first
duly stampt) in the Presence of

Richard Whitmaich

Leigh Tuttle

of the minors are given, as well as the names and parish of their parents and of the guardian (often with his relationship), these documents are of great value to genealogists (see Plate 9).

At Winchester all these Court papers are indexed in typescript, copies being available both at the Society of Genealogists' Library and at Winchester, so that any name can be turned up in a few minutes; but the same indexing may not be found in other dioceses. A calendar of these guardianship papers has been published. (*Winchester Guardianships after 1700*, A.J. Willis [1967].)

CLERGY

Anyone interested in the clergy genealogically should not omit to look at the episcopal records, which include, of course, much about them. They will contain the administrative archives of ordination, licence to curacies, presentation and institution or collation to livings, nominations to perpetual curacies, nonresidence licences, resignations and sequestrations. There may also be caveats against ordination. With the archdeacon's records should be induction mandates.

The most important of these for genealogists are the ordination papers, because they should contain a baptismal or birth certificate. Unfortunately this is sometimes missing, but, if not found with the papers for ordination as deacon, it may be with those for ordination as priest. Apparently both this certificate and testimonials were required on both occasions. The testimonial for deacon's orders will probably be from the college of the ordinand's university, signed by the head and principal fellows. It will give his degree and sometimes mention that he was a scholar or is a fellow of the college. The testimonial for priests' orders is often signed by three neighbouring clergy.

Other records of ordination may be found in other places, but not with this detail. The Bishop's Register (a volume recording his official acts) lists the names at each ordination, usually with their degrees and sometimes their college. There may be an ordination register extant for the period with the archives, and the earlier Visitation Books record the production of orders at the first visitation of a bishop after his consecration. These are often useful to show a move, as they mention date and ordaining bishop for both deacon's and priest's orders, the latter often being in a different diocese from the former.

The other papers referred to above will show movements of the clergy from curacy to curacy or living, and again there may be registers giving this information as well.

The 'Subscription Books' should be mentioned, as these contain the declarations of ordinands of adherence to the Thirty-nine Articles and other requirements of Canon 36 of 1603 and of conformity to the Liturgy of the Church of England. Similar declarations were required on institution to a benefice or licence to a curacy together with a declaration against simony. The extent to which these books have survived will vary in different dioceses, but they are valuable for the signatures of the clergy.

LICENCES TO LAYMEN

The Church was interested in education long before the State took notice of it and, no doubt, as the duties were handed over to laymen the appointments were subject to licence by the bishop. The Church, too, has long been interested in the welfare of the body as well as the soul and still is, as will be seen by their support of medical missions. Physicians, surgeons and midwives were all licensed by the bishop. These licences extend through the 18th century and those for schoolmasters well into the nineteenth.

The value to the genealogist of this licensing is that testimonials were submitted and these give information as to where schoolmasters were teaching and to whom physicians and surgeons were apprenticed (sometimes to their father). Parish clerks and sextons also were licensed by the bishop and produced testimonials.

You can strike lucky and find more than just licences among these records: some of my ancestors were schoolmasters in Yorkshire and a search in the archives of the Archbishop of York unearthed a fascinating series of petitions, dated in 1702, from rival groups of parents in Old Malton. The first complained of the 'Negligence and Corrupt practices' of the current schoolmaster, who even said 'that the Children of those parents who paid him most shall be best taught'; the second asked that the well regarded master of a neighbouring school (my ancestor) be installed instead; the third was a counter-attack to the effect that the present master was a worthy man who taught well and 'never exacts anything for teaching'. The immediate result is not known, but my ancestor did become Old Malton's schoolmaster a few years later, so perhaps his lobbying paid off.

RECORDS OF PAPISTS AND DISSENTERS

Returns of papists from each parish may be found. Though sometimes these are only statistics, there may be lists of names.

Following the Toleration Act of 1688 dissenters were required to apply to the bishop of the diocese or the sessions to have their meeting houses licensed. Applications will give name of owner or occupier of the premises and possibly have other supporters' signatures.

Discovery of the wanted name in either of these categories would turn the searcher to Roman Catholic records, such as those of the Catholic Record Society or to Non-conformist records, such as the non parochial registers (see p.37).

MANORIAL RECORDS

Bishops were in the past large landowners and if an ancestor was in a place found to be within an episcopal manor, the manorial records should be sought out. Manorial records generally are considered in Chapter 13 (pp.92-3).

Wherever the manorial records may be, there may be remaining in the diocesan registry or other repository something of the manorial papers or other deeds and records relating to land.

OTHER RECORDS

There will certainly be other records which will vary from diocese to diocese, probably more of historical than genealogical interest. Such would be visitorship documents (arising from the bishop's position as Visitor to a College), replies from the parishes to Visitation Inquiries, consecration and faculty papers, surrogates' bonds, registrars' accounts, general correspondence, etc.

Chapter 10

The National Archives: Public Record Office

In April 2003 the Public Record Office joined with the Historical Manuscripts Commission to form a new organisation, The National Archives, and the former name is now only used as the place of custody when citing documents in publications. The new name has been used here.

The National Archives is the repository of official records of the Courts of Law and of the Departments of State. For the genealogist it is only in so far as his quarry has come into contact with such official bodies that he will find mention of him there. If he was involved in legal proceedings, or, as a member of the Navy or Army or otherwise, was of interest to a government department, there may be information about him in the public records. Taxation may have brought him to the notice of the Exchequer or transfer of landed property to the Court of Chancery.

The mass of material is enormous, and only a few of the more obvious and important sources of information will be mentioned. These will probably be the first to be investigated unless a definite clue leads elsewhere. If so, its particular direction should be followed; unless there is some such guidance the searcher may find himself lost in a maze of lists, indexes and calendars if he strays beyond the few recognised sources of genealogical information. (See *Tracing your Ancestors in the Public*

Record Office by A. Bevan (6th ed., 2002). An examination of the *Guide to the Contents of the Public Record Office* will give an idea of the immense variety of material. To take just two items, a very small bite out of the whole, there are 17,471 volumes of Ships' Musters for the period 1688-1808 in the Admiralty records and 13,305 volumes of Muster Books (General) amongst the War Office records.

The National Archives (P.R.O.) is based in Kew, where the address is Ruskin Avenue, Kew, Richmond, Surrey TW9 4DU, telephone: 020 8876 3444, www.nationalarchives.gov.uk. However, certain classes of records of particular interest to genealogists are still available in central London, on microfilm or fiche, at the Family Records Centre (as described in Chapters 5, 6 and 8); these are the census returns, P.C.C. wills, death duty registers and nonconformist registers. Of these, the microfilms of the P.C.C. wills and the online and microfiche 1901 census returns are also accessible at Kew.

The National Archives is open Monday, Wednesday and Friday 9.00 am to 5.00 pm, Tuesday 10.00 am to 7.00 pm, Thursday 9.00 am to 7.00 pm and Saturday 9.30 am to 5.00 pm, except on public holidays, and one week's closure for stocktaking, normally in early December. The nearest station is Kew Gardens, a 10-minute walk away, and there are also several bus routes along the nearby South Circular Road, and car-parking space is available. There are full details about visiting Kew on the website, or a map and leaflet can be sent by post.

Before making a visit, it is essential to make sure that the information you want is likely to be in the public records, and to have an idea of the type of records you want to see. The National Archives website includes useful Information Leaflets, indexed under subjects, which can be printed out, and there is also an online catalogue, giving the exact document references, from which you can order up to three documents in advance of your visit, thus saving time when you arrive; this can be done online or by phone. If you do not have access to a computer, I would recommend the beginners' guide, *New to Kew?* by Jane Cox (2001), a 'must' for anyone new to the building and its contents.

There is no charge for searching the records, but a reader's ticket must be obtained, which will be issued on production of suitable ID, such as a passport, driving licence, bank or credit card, or a staff or student ID card. You can pre-register your personal details online up to four weeks before an intended visit and then just show your ID to collect the ticket, or you can complete the application on arrival at the desk in the entrance hall.

The ground floor of the building consists of a spacious foyer, reminiscent of a prosperous corporate headquarters, with a well-stocked bookshop (well worth a browse), cloakrooms and cafe. The Research Enquiries Room, main Reading Rooms, Library and Document Copying Centre are on the first floor, with the Map and Large Document Reading Room on the second floor.

First of all you will need to use the lists and indexes in the Research Enquiries Room to obtain the correct reference for the document(s) you require, if you have not already done this from the online catalogue. The Information Leaflets are also available here, and anyone who still feels completely at sea will find the staff most helpful. The Library has a comprehensive collection of reference books, including Army and Navy Lists, and other books of historical and genealogical interest.

Documents are ordered (three at a time) from computer terminals in the reading rooms, using your reader's ticket and seat number, which must first be obtained from the desk of the reading room. The progress of your order can be checked on the computer at any time, and the documents are then collected from the desk. In some cases there may be no need to wait at all, as documents on microfilm or fiche can be seen at once.

The following are the classes of record most likely to be of interest to the genealogist:

ARMED FORCES AND OTHER SERVICE RECORDS

Army

For officers, there are printed Army Lists from 1754 (WO 65-66), and MS lists from 1702 (WO 64). Some of these can, of course, be seen in other libraries, but the series at Kew will be more complete. Muster Books (WO 10-15), which begin in 1708, list both officers and other ranks by regiment and were used for day to day administration of the regiment; the first entry for a new recruit usually gives his age, place of enlistment and trade. Other main classes of record are Soldiers' Documents (discharge papers), 1760-1913 (WO 97) for soldiers discharged to pension, and Description and Depot Books, 1778-1908 (WO 25 and 67). These should give details of place of birth and career.

It really is essential to know the regiment before attempting to search any of these records, and while the Army Lists provide this information for officers, other sources have to be used for other ranks, in the absence of any family information on the subject.

Beware of the often repeated legend of the ancestor who fought at Waterloo, as this can lead to fruitless hours toiling through Muster Books of all the regiments who were there, only to discover elsewhere that the soldier in question was serving on quite a different front.

The National Archives produces several Information Leaflets on Army records, including *British Army: Officers' Records 1660-1913* and *British Army: Useful Sources for Tracing Soldiers*, which should be consulted for more detailed advice. For tracing First World War soldiers, there is the Debt of Honour Register, online at www.cwgc.org, as described in Chapter 3 (see p.10).

For an ancestor who served in a local militia regiment, there are the Militia Attestation papers, 1806-1915 (WO 96) and the Militia Records, 1759-1925 (WO 68), which should provide details of date and place of birth, and career. There is an information leaflet, *Militia 1757-1914*.

Navy

As with the army, there are printed Navy Lists for officers from 1782, from which the details of a man's career can be discovered. Information on officers can also be found in Lieutenants' Passing Certificates, 1691-1848 (ADM 107), which include a copy of the baptism certificate, and officers' service records from 1756 (ADM 196).

For tracing a rating the name of his ship must be known in order to find him in Ships' Musters, 1688-1878 (ADM 36-41) and Ships' Pay Books, 1691-1856 (ADM 31-35). There are records of seamen's pensions, 1802-1919 (ADM 29), Continuous Service Engagement Books, 1853-1872 (ADM 139) and Seamen's services, 1837-1891 (ADM 188), which provide more information.

There are also a great many seamen's wills and grants of administration, for ordinary sailors as well as officers, from 1786 onwards (ADM 42, 44 and 45); in addition, P.C.C. wills include many wills for seamen and, as already mentioned, can be seen on microfilm.

There are various Information Leaflets available at The National Archives, similar to those for army records, including *Royal Navy: Officers' Service Records* and *Royal Navy: Ratings' Service Records 1667-1923.*

Royal Marines

The Marines were established in 1755, but there are no separate records back to that date. Officers are included in the Navy Lists and their records are included with those of naval officers in the class ADM 196. Other ranks can be traced through Attestations Papers (discharge documents), 1790-1901 (ADM 157) and service records, 1884-1918 (ADM 313 and 159). Once again, there are Information Leaflets, *Royal Marines: Officers' Service Records* and *Royal Marines: Other Ranks' Service Records.*

Merchant Seamen

Until 1853 the details of a merchant seaman's service may be, at least in part, with naval records, as described above, since the same men switched between the services as the situation required.

There are registers of seamen 1835-1844 (BT 112), and also registers of seamen's tickets, 1845-1853 (BT 113), but the registration of seamen stopped in 1857, and after that date there is no easy way of tracing them, although some may appear in the records of the Royal Naval Reserve established in 1859 (ADM 240 and BT 164).

If the name of a seaman's ship or port is known, it may be worth searching crew lists, 1747-1860 (BT 98), and there are also records of apprentices in the merchant fleet, 1824-1953 (BT 150).

There are a number of Information Leaflets, listed in *Merchant Seamen: Records of the RGSS [Registrar General of Shipping and Seamen], A Guide to Leaflets.*

Other Services

Service records of other occupations which came under various government departments are also to be found at The National Archives. These include Coastguards (from 1822), Customs and Excise Officers (from 1820), Dockyard workers (from 1660), Railway Company employees, Metropolitan Police officers (from 1829) and members of the Royal Irish Constabulary (from 1836).

The quantity and quality of records varies from one class to another, but there are Information Leaflets available with more details on each of the above services, and others.

PROFESSIONAL RECORDS

Solicitors and Attorneys

While records of barristers are not at The National Archives (the Inns of Court should be consulted here), there are some documents relating to solicitors and attorneys. These are the Attorneys' and Solicitors' Rolls or Books, which begin in 1729, recording the names of those about to serve their five years as clerks under articles, followed by the Affidavits of Due Execution of Articles of Clerkship, beginning in 1749, which mark the end of that period of training. Further details can be found in the Information Leaflet *Lawyers: Records of Attorneys and Solicitors*.

Naturalisation Certificates

These records, granted to immigrants wishing to become naturalised subjects, begin in 1844 and are in classes HO 1 and HO 334. Prior to that date, denization was more frequent, being less expensive, and denizations were enrolled on Patent Rolls (C66 and C67). Indexes to these, 1509-1800 and 1801-1873, are attached to the list of HO 1. However, most foreign settlers did not bother with these formalities, so cannot be traced through these records. The relevant Information Leaflet is *Naturalization and Citizenship: Grants of British Nationality*.

Apprenticeship Books

Between 1710 and 1811, apprenticeship indentures were subject to tax, and thus records of them are at The National Archives (IR 1, indexed in IR 17). These books record the names, addresses and trades of the masters, and the name of the apprentices, with the date of the indenture; their parents' names are given up to 1752. There are indexes to these records (covering apprentices 1710-1774 and masters 1710-1762) at the Society of Genealogists (see Chapter 11), and further indexes are in preparation. Further details are in the Information Leaflet *Apprenticeship Records as Sources for Genealogy*.

Lay Subsidies

Among Exchequer records are the Subsidy Rolls, which include assessments and accounts for various grants made to the Crown, by Convocation for the clergy, and by the House of Commons for the laity. The latter, the 'lay subsidies', extend up to the reign of Charles II, and are useful to genealogists as they give the names of those who were assessed for taxation, arranged by villages within each hundred (an area of local administration) of every county.

The most useful for the genealogist are the Hearth Tax returns and assessments of 1662-1674 (E 179), the most complete being those for 1664. Some earlier tax returns include names, and this is noted in the class list.

Also of interest are the Land Tax Redemption Office Quotas and Assessments (IR 23), which list all owners of property subject to tax in England and Wales, 1798-1799, arranged by parish. In 1798 this tax became a fixed annual charge and many people purchased exemption; these records sometimes include maps and plans (IR 22 and 24).

There are Information Leaflets, *Taxation Records before 1660* and *The Hearth Tax 1662-1688*.

Inquisitions Post Mortem
On the death of a tenant in chief of the Crown, an enquiry was held before a jury, who had to swear to the lands held by the tenant, and the name, age and relationship of the next heir; this process continued up to 1660, when feudal tenures were abolished. The records of these inquisitions are among Chancery, Exchequer and Court of Wards records and are indexed. They are, however, of little relevance except in the case of substantial landowning families. There is an Information Leaflet *Inquisitions Post Mortem, Henry III-Charles I: Land Holders and their Heirs*.

Feet of Fines
When conveyance of landed property was in a very rudimentary stage somebody seems to have discovered that if there could be

a dispute at law about the ownership of land, and that dispute was settled by the Court, first-class evidence as to ownership was thereby provided. Hence, it seems, arose the series of 'Fines' (so-called because they made a final end to the dispute, the general opening to the Foot of Fine being *'Hec est finalis concordia ...'*). The 'Fine' was an agreement or composition of a suit (usually fictitious) made between the parties with the consent of the Court and by which the transfer or settlement of freehold property was determined. There were several steps in the procedure, but the 'Foot of Fine' set out the terms of the agreement. For an example see p.114. Where several members of the same family were concerned, their relationship would normally be given. Feet of Fines are in Latin until the reign of George II, after which they are in English, and continue until 1833.

Some indexes and calendars to Feet of Fines have been published by various local societies, and these are the easiest means of reference. There is a useful article on the subject, 'Feet of Fines', by M. Tatchell (*Genealogists' Magazine*, vol. 19, no. 10, June 1979, pp.347-9), and an Information Leaflet *Feet of Fines 1182-1833*.

Law Court Records
The records of the various law courts are to be found at The National Archives. If the family has been known to have engaged in a lawsuit, information may be found there in the form of affidavits lodged and judgements, with other papers such as private deeds. However, searching all these classes of records is a lengthy process, and is not something to be undertaken on the off-chance that something might turn up, unless all other avenues have drawn a blank, and even then only if the family concerned was reasonably prosperous and likely to have engaged in a lawsuit.

Among Law Court Records, the following should be specially mentioned:

Chancery Proceedings

A good deal of litigation, largely in relation to property or money, came before the Equity side of the Court of Chancery in the form of petitions (or 'bills'), with their answers and depositions. Calendars of the early suits have been printed, but for later ones only MS calendars are available. These are classified under the names of the Six Clerks, and up to 1714 give bundle reference number, names of plaintiffs and defendants, date and subject matter of the suit, and name of the county concerned. These particulars are grouped together under the initial letter of the principal plaintiff's name, and one may therefore find a suit where this is known. But it is not so easy to trace the name of a defendant or associated plaintiff. It is, of course, necessary to search the lists of all the Six Clerks, unless it is known by which the suit was handled. In cases where several members of the same family are either joint or opposite parties, relationship may be established from these suits. After 1714 the lists only give names of parties without any county, so the help of locality in eliminating the unwanted is not available. A further problem is that papers dealing with a single case are not filed together, but with other documents of the same type from different cases, so it is very difficult to follow through one particular suit.

The value to genealogists of these proceedings is, however, not so much in the bills and answers as in the depositions of witnesses which are filed with the papers. The deponents give their age and place of residence and sometimes other genealogical information. For names in these the Bernau Index, on microfilm at the Society of Genealogists (see Chapter 11) is worth consulting, as it includes names in Chancery Proceedings 1714-1800, two series of Depositions and parts of other classes of records.

While on the subject of Chancery, many families have stories of untold millions awaiting a claimant 'in Chancery'. It is true that since 1876 solicitors have deposited money for which they were unable to trace legatees or next of kin, and lists of these have been published as supplements to the *London Gazette* from 1893, which can be consulted at The National Archives. However, successful claims to one of these funds are extremely rare, and the sums of money involved are mostly very insignificant. There is an Information Leaflet *Money (Funds) in Court*. In addition, a new database of all dormant funds can now be searched free of charge at the Court Funds Office, 22 Kingsway, London WC2B 6LE; further details are on their website www. courtservice.gov.uk/cfo/dormant.htm.

Exchequer Depositions
Similar depositions to those in Chancery are found in the Court of Exchequer records. There is a printed calendar and here supplementary information is available to trace deponents, with a typed list of deponents in each case for the period 1559-1695, the cases being arranged in groups according to locality, with the county given in a marginal heading. This is also available at the Society of Genealogists, with MS slips for the later period up to 1800.

Useful guides to these legal records are the Information Leaflets *Chancery Proceedings: Equity Suits before 1558* and *Equity Suits from 1558*, and *Equity Proceedings in the Court of Exchequer*, and an article, 'Genealogical Resources in Chancery Records', P.W Coldham (*Genealogists' Magazine*, vol.XIX, pp.345-57 and vol.XX, pp.257-60).

* * *

Some of the items mentioned above are approaching more advanced work, but it seems advisable to draw attention to their existence. The main interest of the beginner at The National Archives will be in the records of the armed forces and other government employees and perhaps apprenticeship books, in addition to those records which can be consulted in central London and are the basis for most genealogical research.

There are, however, public records elsewhere, such as county and municipal archives, as well as a very large number of printed sources and transcriptions of original records, all of which can provide vital clues for family history.

There are also other important repositories for genealogists, such as the Library of the Society of Genealogists, for both national and local material, and county or city libraries for items of local interest. Next, therefore, must be examined the resources of libraries, which will cover not only manuscripts but the vast collections of available printed books.

Chapter 11

The Society of Genealogists' Library

This is one of the most important repositories in the country for any genealogist, containing a unique and ever-growing collection of material, much of it available on open shelves and online.

The Library is at the Society's headquarters, 14 Charterhouse Buildings, Goswell Road, London EC1M 7BA (telephone: 020 7702 5480 or 020 7702 5485 – library enquiries), www.sog.org.uk. The opening hours are Tuesday, Wednesday, Friday and Saturday 10.00 am to 6.00 pm, Thursday 10.00 am to 8.00 pm; the Society is closed on Mondays. There is also an annual 'closed week', currently the first full week in February, when the library is closed to visitors for various necessary changes and improvements.

Membership of the Society, giving free access to the library, a quarterly magazine and other privileges including a varied programme of lectures, courses and visits, costs £40 a year plus an initial joining fee of £10. Non-members can also use the library on payment of a fee. The Society no longer has a bookshop at headquarters, but it still sells its own publications, which can also be ordered online. Its mobile bookshop continues to be a familiar sight at many family history fairs around the country.

Before going to the Society, it is essential to have collected as much information as possible from family members – birth, marriage and death certificates, and census returns, as described in Chapters 1, 4 and 5 – and to have some idea of what you are looking for. A copy of the Floor Guide to the library is available free to new members and those making general enquiries, which lists all the major holdings of the library with their locations. The following is a brief summary of the most important sources available on the shelves or on microfiche and online in the Society's library, but obviously it cannot be exhaustive, and when a series of publications is mentioned, it must not be assumed to be complete.

INTERNET SUITE

This gives free access to a number of major online sources, including:

English Origins website (www.englishorigins.com), which contains the larger indexes of the Society, such as Boyd's Marriage Index, Marriage Licence Allegations Index, London Apprenticeship Index and PCC Wills, and is being expanded all the time (see below for further details of these indexes)

FamilySearch for the International Genealogical Index and census return entries (www.familysearch.org)

Partial indexes to births, marriages and deaths 1837-1902 (www.freebmd.rootsweb.org)

Debt of Honour Register (www.cwgc.org)

(Further details of these and other websites are given in Chapter 3.)

REGIONAL

This part of the library is arranged alphabetically by English counties (as existing in 1837), with separate sections for Wales, Scotland and Ireland. The records include:

Items relating to the whole county, such as histories, bibliographies, maps, newspapers, record office guides and wills

More local items, including parish histories, church guides and
other material on particular places

Parish registers and those of non-Church of England denominations: the Society holds the largest collection of copies in the
country, printed, typescript, manuscript and on film or fiche
(see *County Sources at the Society of Genealogists* - volumes for
each county); they are listed online at www. sog.org.uk/prc

Monumental Inscriptions, copied from gravestones in countless
numbers of churches, churchyards and other burial grounds

Census Returns: those for 1841-1861 on microfilm, 1881 census
and index on CD-ROM or fiche, 1901 census and index online, and indexes for other years

Trade Directories from the 1770s onwards, and Poll Books (lists
of voters at parliamentary elections) between 1694 and 1832,
with some later ones

Local collections: the results of research carried out by former
members and including the Snell Collection (Berkshire), the
Rogers Collection (Cornwall), the Campling Collection (Norfolk) and Boyd's Inhabitants of London and London Burials.

TRADES AND PROFESSIONS

Apprentices and their Masters in Great Britain: a typescript
index to the series of records at The National Archives covering the years 1710-1774 (due to be added to the English
Origins website)

School registers and histories (mainly for grammar and public
schools)

University and college registers and histories

Army Lists from 1661-1714 and 1740 to recent times

Navy Lists from 1756, and naval biographical dictionaries

Air Force Lists from 1936

Clergy lists 1066 onwards

Law Lists 1812-1976

Registers of Admissions to the Inns of Court
Medical registers and directories from 1845
Teachers Registration Council Registers 1902-1948
Trinity House Petitions 1787-1890: applications for charitable
assistance by merchant seamen and their families

BOYD'S MARRIAGE INDEX

This consists of over 500 bound typescript volumes, and is also available on the English Origins website. It contains entries, arranged alphabetically under men's and (in most cases) women's surnames, compiled from transcribed parish registers available at the time it was prepared, covering the years 1538-1837. Obviously it is not complete, but it does contain about seven million names, and can provide useful leads, if not the actual marriage required. It is limited to particular counties: Cambridgeshire, Cornwall, Cumberland (to 1700 only), Derbyshire, Devon, co. Durham, Essex, Gloucestershire, Lancashire, Middlesex and London, Norfolk, Northumberland, Shropshire, Somerset, Suffolk and Yorkshire, as well as a Miscellaneous section for other counties. The parishes included in the Index are listed in *A List of Parishes in Boyd's Marriage Index* (reprinted 1994).

OTHER INDEXES AND COLLECTIONS

These are mostly on microfilm, fiche or CD-ROM, and include:
Civil Registration: England and Wales 1837-1925, Scotland 1855-1920, Guernsey 1840-1966, New Zealand 1840-1920, Australia to *c.*1900
Wills: P.C.C. 1383-1800 and some years to 1857, Estate Duty wills 1796-1857, Principal Probate Registry 1858-1930
Marriage licence allegations: Faculty Office & Vicar General 1632-1851
The Times: birth, marriage & death announcements 1816-1920 and indexes 1785-1920

Bernau Index: litigants in Chancery and other court depositions at The National Archives. There is a useful guide to this: *How to Use the Bernau Index* by H. Sharp (2nd ed., 2000)

Great Card Index: this contains several million slips, arranged by surname with references to original sources, such as Parish registers, marriage licences, legal records and monumental inscriptions; it is a bit of a lucky dip, but most surnames are represented, and the Index offers a fair guide to their distribution

Dwelly Index: West Country material

Whitehead Index: East Anglian references

Fawcett Index: Clergy and North Country families

Glencross Index: Cornwall and Devon sources

Macleod Collection: working papers of two Scottish genealogists for several hundred Scottish families

Wagner Collection: Huguenot pedigrees

Colyer-Fergusson, Hyamson & Mordy Collections: Jewish material

INTERNATIONAL GENEALOGICAL INDEX

This is described more fully in Chapter 6 (p.30). The Society has the 1992 edition on fiche, and the latest edition is available online in the Internet Suite.

The Library also has collections of material relating to families in the United States, India, the West Indies, Australia, New Zealand and Canada, as well as a comprehensive collection of reference books on genealogy, heraldry, the peerage and royal families, biographical dictionaries (including the *Dictionary of National Biography* on CD-ROM) and various genealogical periodicals. The publications of several specialist organisations are also available, such as those of the Harleian Society, Jewish Historical Society, Huguenot Society, Society of Friends and Historical Manuscripts Commission.

Chapter 12
Libraries and Record Offices

Other libraries will vary considerably in size and scope. There are general libraries such as the British Library, the Bodleian at Oxford, or the Cambridge University Library, and local libraries in each city or town, the larger of which, while having a special section of local books, approximate to a general library. There are also specialist libraries such as those of learned societies like the Society of Antiquaries, certain government departments with special spheres of administration or county record offices which will concentrate on books relating to the particular area. County, city and borough reference libraries are free, but the libraries of societies are mostly restricted to their members, though facilities will usually be allowed to research students with or without payment of a fee.

Apart from the specific requirement of the Copyright Act for delivery of a copy of every publication to the British Library, certain other libraries have under various enactments been entitled to claim a copy. A clause in the Copyright Act of 1911 requires delivery on request of a copy of every publication to the Bodleian Library, the Cambridge University Library, the National Libraries of Scotland and Wales, and the Library of Trinity College, Dublin. Such a request is, in fact, mostly made, and in any case publishers often send copies automatically without waiting for a request, so these libraries should have all British publications of value to genealogists, at any rate since 1911.

One must naturally adapt one's use of a library to the particular case in hand. It is no use looking at old numbers of *Landed Gentry* or *The Gentleman's Magazine* when dealing with a working man's family; on the other hand, a directory or local newspaper might in such a case be useful. One must investigate to see what can be found in a general library rather than expect to be told what to look for.

An examination of the lending library section may provide something interesting. The reference for books on genealogy, following the decimal classification commonly used by libraries, is 929, so the relevant books can quickly be found. Most reference libraries have a classified index, often on microfiche, and the section on Genealogy might be looked through, as some books may be out on loan and so not seen on the shelves. Whilst such searching in a public library will most likely not produce an answer to the immediate genealogical quest, it widens one's knowledge of the possibilities and so indirectly is a help. Without a knowledge of the contents of all the main libraries one cannot give any general guide, but one or two categories might be mentioned.

A CITY OR BOROUGH LIBRARY

As mentioned in Chapter 3, one of the best ways to discover the whereabouts of local authority libraries, and a guide to their contents, is the website www.familia.org.uk, which lists all such libraries in the UK and Ireland, with details of their addresses and opening hours, plus a list of all their holdings of genealogical interest. Obviously it is best to check with an individual library before making a long journey, in case the details on the website have changed, or it is temporarily closed for any reason.

In any big municipal library will be found all the reference books of a general nature likely to be required, e.g., *Dictionary of National Biography*, atlases and gazetteers, standard histories, etc. In addition to standard works, most big public libraries now have a collection of genealogical material (such as census returns, parish registers and the IGI) on microfilm or fiche, but normally relating only to the local area, so your own local library will not be of much help if your ancestors lived in another part of the country. Other resources are likely to include directories, poll books, periodicals, newspapers and printed copies of local records.

A public library, particularly that of a county town or other large centre, is fairly certain to have a good collection of topographical literature on its own district. It may be worthwhile paying a special visit to the library of a district in which lived the family being traced. Not only may there be books of local interest, perhaps privately printed or otherwise rare, but there may sometimes be manuscript records to be found. The public library in a large town may have a separate department of archives holding collections of the papers of local families as well as, possibly, deposited parish records. Though one may not be searching for gentry, some member of such families as a magistrate or churchwarden may have retained or acquired a collection of documents bearing on his duties. For instance, in Sheffield a long list of apprenticeships and a list of poor-law papers have been prepared from such a source.

Finally, a borough library may well have the records of the meetings of various bodies which administered the borough, the rolls of its freemen and accounts of its financial officers. The borough may have supervised the placing of apprentices in which case there may be apprenticeship records.

GUILDHALL LIBRARY

The City of London's Guildhall Library (Aldermanbury, EC2P 2EJ, tel: 020 7332 1868 for Printed Books, 020 7332 1863 for

Manuscripts, www.cityoflondon.gov.uk/leisure_heritage/libraries) deserves special mention as one of the principal city libraries with some material of more than local interest. The Library does not make a charge, nor is there any need for a reader's ticket, and its opening hours are Monday to Saturday 9.30 am-5.00 pm. The archives include records of the Freemen of the City of London and of the City livery companies, including apprenticeship and admissions registers. It is worth remembering that before the 19th century all who practised a trade or craft within the City had to be both Liverymen and Freemen. However, many Freemen who did not work in the City were not livery company members, so they may only appear in one set of records. Furthermore, many liverymen had their origins outside London (Dick Whittington being the most famous example), and a father's place of residence is often given in apprenticeship books, which can provide a vital clue. A useful guide to these records is *My Ancestors were Freemen of the City of London* by V.E. Aldous (Society of Genealogists, 1999).

The Library also holds the original registers of virtually every City parish, and also wills proved in the Archdeaconry and Commissary Courts of London, as well as many London marriage licence allegations.

In addition, there are comprehensive collections of directories and poll books and, of course, a huge collection of printed and MS material relating to the City of London, including letters and other private papers and matters concerning ceremonial and the City Corporation.

COUNTY RECORD OFFICES

These can easily be located through the guidebook *Record Offices: How to Find Them* by J. Gibson and H. Peskett (9th ed. 2002), or via a website such as the Historical Manuscripts Commission, now part of The National Archives (www. nationalarchives.gov.uk). Every record office has its own website, which will include such basic information as location and opening hours; many also include an online catalogue. They will mainly be used for their collections of parish registers, wills and bishops' transcripts and marriage licence allegations, as well as maps, manorial records, estate records, old photographs and family papers.

In addition, the records of the local county authority will be in the county record office. One important category of records which may be found there are the order books and other records of the Courts of Quarter Sessions for the county. These might be either of the full Court sitting four times a year or of the country magistrates who to a limited extent were empowered to make orders. Besides a restricted jurisdiction in criminal cases, the Quarter Sessions exercised a kind of supervision over local administration before the days of the County Councils, County Courts or the Local Government Board. Hence came before it such matters as bastardy cases, breaches of apprenticeship indentures and disputes over parish settlement (see pp.39-41, all of which may yield genealogical information.

There will also be the records of the proceedings of the local authority, with accounts of their financial officers, sometimes even with the vouchers for payments. Records of such transactions as the granting of licences, benefactions or endowments may be found as well as details of the general activities of the district, such as charitable and official functions. Much of this, if not strictly of genealogical value, may be of interest in extending information about known members of a family.

Most county record offices now produce leaflets about records which are of interest to family historians, and there are guides to their holdings of parish registers, wills and so on (see the Bibliography).

SPECIALIST LIBRARIES

If one comes on some particular technical or otherwise specialised point one should turn for assistance to the library of the appropriate society. Many government departments have libraries covering their own field, and these may be found of assistance.

If an ancestor is known to have belonged to a particular profession, or to have been a beneficiary of a charitable institution, information may well be found by investigating the archives of the body concerned, starting with a letter of enquiry to the librarian. Obviously the easiest way to find the appropriate organisation is through a search engine on the internet, but a good reference library should also be able to help with tracking down addresses and telephone numbers if you do not have internet access yourself.

FAMILY HISTORY CENTRES

There are Family History Centres in every part of the country, organised by the Church of Jesus Christ of Latter-day Saints, and they can be found on their website, www.familysearch.org by clicking on the 'Library' tab, then 'Family History Centers'. There is usually more than one for each county (Kent, for instance, has four), but their opening hours vary considerably and are often very limited, so you should check carefully before making a visit.

Not surprisingly, they hold copies of the IGI, and also microfiche copies of the indexes to births, marriages and deaths, and much other material. It is also possible to order copies of any English genealogical records (including a great many parish registers) which have been microfilmed by the Church, for viewing at a particular Centre. These can be identified in the online Family History Library Catalogue, from which you can obtain the film references that will enable you to order the film you wish to search.

As they are not confined to purely local records, Family History Centres can have more to offer the genealogist than some local libraries, especially for initial searches.

Chapter 13

Other Sources

In this chapter something will be said of a variety of sources of information, some of which have been mentioned only incidentally in the previous chapters.

MANORIAL RECORDS

A vast quantity of manorial records survive in various record offices and collections around the country. A register of these holdings, the Manorial Documents Register, is kept by The National Archives: Historical Manuscripts Commission, currently at Quality House, Quality Court, Chancery Lane, London WC2A 1HP, telephone: 020 7242 1198, but from the end of 2003 at the Public Record Office, Ruskin Avenue, Kew, Richmond, Surrey TW9 4DU, www.nationalarchives.gov.uk. Unfortunately very few counties' records are indexed online at present, so a visit, or enquiry by letter, phone or e-mail will almost certainly be needed. The current opening hours are Monday to Friday 9.30-5.00, but after the move to Kew they will be as given on p.70.

The names of the manor or manors in any particular parish can be found in the relevant volume of the Victoria County History (more details about the coverage of this mammoth work, which originally started in 1899, are on the website www. englandspast.net), or in other local history books, which should be available in large reference libraries or record offices.

The main items of interest to genealogists are the court rolls, the records of the courts held, usually with the steward presiding. Important information is given in these, as they include admissions to tenancies on the death of a tenant. Normally the heir was admitted on payment of a fine and his relationship to the deceased is recorded. The Court also had a disciplinary function as is illustrated by the court roll reproduced in plate 10 (p.94) where it will be seen that various tenants were 'presented' for not keeping their houses and other buildings in repair.

NEWSPAPERS

The national collection of newspapers is held by the British Library, and kept at its Newspaper Library, Colindale Avenue, London NW9 5HE, telephone: 020 7412 7353, www.bl.uk/collections/newspapers.html, but record offices and libraries often hold collections of local interest. The Cyndi's List website has a page devoted to newspapers at www.cyndislist.com/newspapr. htm, and there are also links to local newspapers from the relevant Genuki county pages at www.genuki.org.uk. Obviously, in view of the sheer quantity of material, there is very little yet available online.

One must remember that in the earlier days of newspapers – the 18th and 19th centuries – facilities for delivery were not what they are today. There was no London paper delivered to the provinces on the day of issue. Local papers, therefore, contained the national as well as the local news, with the result that the latter was often limited to a few paragraphs about each principal town in the district. From quite early issues there are records of births, marriages and deaths, though, again, to a very much smaller extent than today. Local advertisements are sometimes of interest with particulars of properties, public announcements etc.

MAGAZINES

Two invaluable current journals are *The Genealogists' Magazine* and *Family History News and Digest*, free to members of the Society of Genealogists and the Federation of Family History

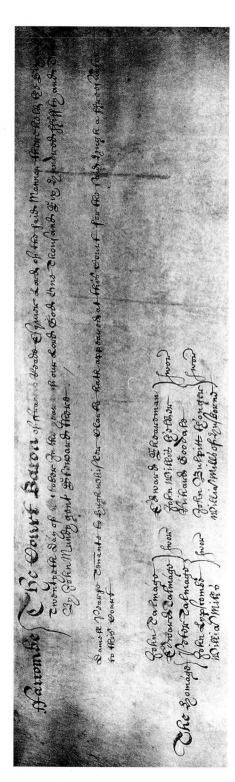

Plate 10 A Manorial Court Roll
(from the British Library, Add. Charters 5077)
(By permission of the British Library)

TRANSCRIPT OF PLATE 10

Faccombe

The Court Baron of Francis Reade Esquier Lord of the said Mannar there held the Six and Twentyeth Day of October In the yeare of our Lord God One Thousand Six Hundred Fiffty and Three by John Mundy gent Steward there

Daniell Pearse Tenante to Hugh Whisler Clarke hath appeared at this Court for the said Hugh a Freesuitor to this Court

The Homage	John Talmage		Edward Sheareman	
	Edward Talmage	sworn	John Willis th'elder	sworn
	Peter Talmage }		Richard Goodale	}
	John Lypscombe	sworn	John Bulpitt th'onger [the younger]	sworn
	Willia[m] Mills		Willia[m] Mills of Husborne	

Allsoe they order That none shall put more than sixty sheepe upon a yard Lands into the Comons according to a former order upon payne of forfeiting for ev[er]y sheepe for ev[er]y weeke iiijd.

The note of the Tenants Houses that are out of repayre followeth

Rob[er]t Browne his Barne & his out Houses want groundpining groundsells walling Rafters & Thatching

John Bulpitt of Kember his House wants groundpining groundsells walling & Thatching

Jo: [John] Willis th'onger (Widow Goodfellowes tenant) the dwelling House wants Thatching the Barne at the end groundpining

The Widow Hollyers Barne wants Walling (This is a Leassehold)

Edward Shearmans House at Upstreete (in the poss[essi]on of Seare) wants Thatching walling and groundpining

Edward Haywards Barne (W[illia]m Mills the Tenant) wants a groundsell (Leasse)

Richard Goodales Maulting House wants Walling

Societies respectively; the latter is also sold at the Family Records Centre, the National Archives and some record offices. The National Archives produces its own bi-monthly magazine, *Ancestors*, available in its shop and at the Family Records Centre or by subscription. Other widely available monthly magazines for genealogists include *Family Tree Magazine*, *Family History Monthly* and *Practical Family History*. All of these contain fascinating and informative articles on a wide range of topics relating to family history, as well as useful notices and advertisements, and are worth looking through and buying on an occasional basis, even if you do not take out a subscription.

Journals from the 18th and early 19th centuries, such as *The Gentleman's Magazine*, are of little general interest as they relate mainly to the nobility and gentry, but some are now being made available online, as the Internet Library of Early Journals (see www.bodley.ox.ac.uk/ilej).

DIRECTORIES

These date mostly from the 19th century, and are a useful source if your ancestors were tradespeople, especially if you are trying to find an address for a family in the census returns. By going through a run of them, you can establish the dates of family businesses and changes of address. Many tradesmen are also listed in the 'Private Residents' section, which includes retired business-owners and those whose home address was not 'over the shop', as well as what we now think of as the upper classes (nobility, gentry, clergy, army and navy officers).

The Family Records Centre has a selection of directories for London and Middlesex only in the Reference area to help with searches in census returns, and the Society of Genealogists has a large collection for every part of the country (see p.83), as do record offices and reference libraries for their own localities. A number are available on CD-ROM, and a few are even online in transcription or as scanned images. The Genuki website (www.genuki.org.uk) gives links to these on its county pages.

POLL BOOKS

Poll books give a return of those who voted at Parliamentary elections and therefore give a fairly full list of the property owners of the district, the vote being then entirely based on property qualification. They are mostly of late 18th- and early 19th-century date, though a few of earlier date survive in some counties. The collections at the Society of Genealogists and Guildhall Library in London have already been mentioned (pages 83 and 89), and local record offices and reference libraries normally have good holdings.

MONUMENTAL INSCRIPTIONS

This term (abbreviated by the genealogist to M.I.s) covers both gravestones in churchyards or inside churches and memorial tablets not at the place of burial. These sometimes give information as to dates of death, names of husband or wife, children, etc. Where the deceased had recently moved from another place, they sometimes give his former place of residence – or, if erected there, they give the place to which he had moved. The tracing of a family move is one of the constant problems in genealogical research. M.I.s mostly refer to the gentry, so one cannot expect to find memorials to the humbler families in the village church.

Churchyard memorials of the 18th century are often illegible now, though some of good stone in sheltered places can still be deciphered, if carefully examined, and others, the inscriptions of which have been re-cut, are reasonably clear. When the parish of the family is known, the churchyard should be visited with this possibility in view. For the earlier 19th century, before the establishment of the General Register Office, they make a useful supplement to information in the parish register, and even after that date they may amplify a death certificate.

In some cases, a question of identity has been solved by information on a gravestone. A case in point is that of Jane Pink, born about 1771/2, who married Henry Barton in Colchester, Essex, both being Wesleyan Methodists; it seemed likely that she was the daughter of William Pink, a member of the Wesleyan Chapel in Colchester, but there were no baptismal records for the 1770s. However, a Jane, daughter of William and Mary Pink, was baptised at the Independent Chapel there in 1772, and a Jane Pink married Francis Exton in 1799 – which Jane was which? Fortunately copies of the M.I.s for the Independent Chapel were found, which included adjacent inscriptions to William and Mary Pink, and to Francis and Jane Exton. This showed that the Jane baptised in 1772 was the one who married Francis Exton, and could not have been the one who married Henry Barton; the latter was presumably the daughter of the Wesleyan William Pink.

There are records of M.I.s both in print and in manuscript. Inquiry should always be made at the local record office or large reference library, as a copy may have been deposited there; the largest collection in the country is at the Society of Genealogists' Library in London. A guide to what is available online is *Monumental Inscriptions on the Web*, compiled by S.A. Raymond (2002).

There is also a project, the National Burial Index, compiled by the Federation of Family History Societies, and produced on CD-ROM (2001), which includes more than 5.4 million names, mainly from the early 19th century, from over 4,300 churchyards and cemeteries in England and Wales, although coverage varies between counties. It can be seen at the Family Records Centre and some other record offices.

BIOGRAPHY

Many of the public schools have printed registers of their pupils, in some cases going back to the 15th century. The information given varies: sometimes it includes name and occupation of father. The Universities of Oxford and Cambridge have such printed lists, known as *Alumni Oxonienses* and *Alumni Cantabrigienses*. Some of the other Universities and each of the Inns of Court have similar lists. Often a brief biographical note will be found in these registers.

For officers in the services, old Navy or Army Lists will be found useful, and there are Clerical and Medical Directories for the clergy and doctors, while other professions (such as solicitors, architects, surveyors and engineers) all have their own professional bodies whose libraries would be worth consulting. There are even printed biographical works available in larger reference libraries for some of these professions, as well as for painters, sculptors, writers and musicians.

If an ancestor held some official position, such as sheriff, justice of the peace, mayor or alderman, appropriate lists can be seen in the relevant record office or public library.

Of course anyone who achieved fame or notoriety may well appear in the *Dictionary of National Biography* (a new 60-volume and online edition, due in September 2004, will include 50,000 biographies), or *Who Was Who*, which reprints entries from *Who's Who* from 1897 onwards, after the subjects' deaths.

Genealogical information on the peerage and gentry can be found in *Burke's Peerage* and *Burke's Landed Gentry*, but these publications only cover a tiny proportion of the population.

Guilds and Trade Associations

Since the formation of guilds of merchants in early days there have been trade associations of various kinds. Such bodies as the various livery companies of the City of London, each of which relates to a trade, have records of their proceedings, admissions to their register, apprenticeships and so on. In the case of anybody in trade or business in or near London the records of the relevant livery company should be looked up. They may be at Guildhall Library (see p.89) or still in the custody of the company.

County record offices or reference libraries will be able to give information about local guilds or associations which existed, and the survival of their records.

FAMILY HISTORIES AND PEDIGREES

Numerous family histories have been compiled over the years and these mostly include pedigrees. Some may be unreliable, particularly those which, to cover a gap in the evidence, say 'from whom was descended ...'. It should be fairly easy to see whether each step is properly substantiated. Pedigrees will also be found in manuscript in various libraries and record offices. All these records again refer to the gentry and do not help the humbler families.

If there is any possibility that a right to armorial bearings has been recorded, the College of Arms should be consulted (enquiries should be addressed to the Officer in Waiting, College of Arms, Queen Victoria Street, London EC4V 4BT). Its records are not open to the public but for a fee a search can be made to establish whether any family of a particular name is on record as entitled to a coat of arms.

If a right to arms is to be established it will be necessary to prove direct male descent from one of the families whose arms are in the official records of the College of Arms, and to register the pedigree at the College. Every statement in the pedigree must be supported by legally acceptable evidence from contemporary records, and the pedigree will be carefully scrutinised by two of the officers at the College before being accepted. The officers (the Kings, Heralds and Pursuivants of Arms), though appointed by the Crown, are mainly dependent on the fees paid for the services they render: those who consult them must, therefore, expect to pay on a scale suitable for professional experts.

LEASES AND TITLE DEEDS

These may provide useful information about a family and its movements, though they are not often likely to give direct evidence of descent. Such records are now usually deposited in county record offices, who should be consulted about surviving records for a particular locality.

MAPS

Old maps are useful in identifying the hundreds or wapentakes (areas of local administration) into which a county was divided; these are needed in searching some early records. A map of the area where a family lived should always be studied (reprints of the first edition of the Ordnance Survey maps are useful here), as the configuration of the ground and directions of roads may provide a clue to movements. One must remember that transport was very restricted, even in the early 19th century, and that a horse, with or without a cart, was the principal means of transport for any distance that could not be walked.

Tithe maps, produced as a result of the Tithe Commutation Act of 1836, are large-scale maps giving names of landowners and occupiers with details of their holdings and land cultivation. Copies are at The National Archives (P.R.O.) and in county record offices.

REFERENCE BOOKS

Some of the most useful reference books are the various printed indexes to records. The Harleian Society and the British Record Society in particular have each issued a series of volumes including indexes to wills, marriage licence allegations and copies of parish registers. The catalogue of the British Library or of any library which has a series should be looked at to see whether there are any indexes referring to the county or diocese in which the searcher is interested. There are also officially published indexes to some of the public records.

Another category often referred to is books of topography, particularly the older ones which give information about old names of places, administrative boundaries etc., at the time of their publication. It is often useful to know which hundred or wapentake a parish was in. Old histories will be found of each county, and *The Victoria County History* covers most counties. For many counties the publication is in several volumes and in some cases the series is not yet complete. In the case of London, *The Greater London Council Survey of London* may help to fill a gap.

Many counties have or have had archaeological societies which include genealogy among their interests, or even a more specialised parish register society. These societies have usually published their transactions, as well as produced particular volumes on special subjects. There are also contributions from individuals who have written the history of a parish and included a copy of, or extracts from, the parish registers and other documents, or who have even made a survey of some particular branch of records over a wider field.

COMMUNICATION AND EXCHANGE

Genealogists are usually delighted to make contact with others working on the same name, or even better, the same family, and previously unknown relations can sometimes be discovered. You can also share your information, perhaps providing someone else with material new to them, or learning of an undiscovered source that provides a vital clue for your own family history.

Obviously the main means of making such connections now is via the internet, which can put you in touch with people in this country or on the other side of the world in no time at all.

This has been discussed in Chapter 3 (see pp.9-10), where the most appropriate websites are suggested, in particular Genuki (www.genuki.org.uk), but even the big search engines can occasionally turn up something of interest.

I struck lucky with my grandmother's family simply through Google (her surname is an unusual one so I thought it was worth a try), and found a website created by another descendant of the same family, with a pedigree going back to the 17th century. Admittedly I had already covered the same ground the hard way 20 years earlier, but it was reassuring to see that we had followed the same line, and I did discover a lot of extra details which I had not followed up in my own searches. I was even put in touch with a previously unknown third cousin, whose very elderly mother remembered going to my father's 21st birthday party in the 1930s!

One Name Societies have also been mentioned (see p.10), and as well as having a website (www.one-name.org), further details can also be obtained from the Guild of One-Name Studies, Box G, 14 Charterhouse Buildings, Goswell Road, London EC1M 7BA.

There are now many local Family History Societies, nearly all of which are affiliated to the Federation of Family History Societies, whose Administrator can be contacted at PO Box 2425, Coventry CV5 6YX; their website is www.ffhs.org.uk, which also has a link to their online bookshop, stocking a huge range of books, CD-ROMs and other material of genealogical interest; the website also includes 'Help' leaflets to assist in research. The Federation produces a twice-yearly journal, which includes articles from local societies' magazines, and notices of lectures, family history fairs, conferences, open days and educational courses. It also organises many projects, such as the National Burial Index mentioned above (p.98), indexes to census returns, county marriage indexes and transcriptions of monumental inscriptions. The local societies themselves organise lectures, educational and other events and act as local meeting places for all those interested in family history.

PROFESSIONAL HELP

A professional genealogist can either be asked to undertake specific searches, or can be given a wider brief and asked to carry out as much work as possible to trace a particular family within specified financial limits. This can be invaluable to people no longer living in the same part of the country as their ancestors, as a researcher in the area will have specialist knowledge of local sources and local history, which could, in the long run, save much time and expense.

Those wishing to consult a professional genealogist are advised to consult the list published by the Association of Genealogists and Record Agents (A.G.R.A.), which gives the names, addresses and special interests of members all over the country. Copies may be seen in most record offices and libraries, or may be obtained from the Hon. Secretaries, 29 Badgers Close, Horsham, West Sussex RH12 5RU or their website, www. agra.org.uk.

Chapter 14
Conclusion

There is no conclusion to genealogy; even if one line of descent comes to an apparent dead end, there are others to be pursued. The scope is infinite, as searches can be made for the ancestry of all four grandparents, then their parents, and so on, almost *ad infinitum*. Even the most hopeless case should never be completely abandoned, as some hitherto unknown records may come to light, or information from an unexpected source may turn up, perhaps quite by chance, and this can be the long-awaited breakthrough.

Another approach, when a family tree has been traced back for two or three hundred years, is to try to flesh out the bare bones of the line of descent, using some of the other local records mentioned in Chapters 7, 9, 12 and 13.

It should be fairly straightforward to trace a pedigree back to the early 1800s (although even this has been known to cause problems), but before the 19th century there are many obstacles, such as the removal of a family from one place to another or a gap in the records. At this date so many official sources are lacking that almost anything *might* provide a clue; skill lies in seeing the possibilities, weighing them, picking out the probabilities with some idea of their relative likelihood, and testing them systematically and thoroughly.

The main problems for most of those who want to trace their family trees are distance from the sources to be investigated and/

or lack of time. These can be met to a certain extent by carrying out the research by correspondence, but naturally this is less satisfactory than direct searching.

Sometimes a half-and-half method may be used: to pursue the subject oneself where practicable, but employing a local searcher for particular tasks, such as examining a certain parish register for a given period, or making abstracts of a number of possible wills. There is, of course, the alternative of handing over the whole problem to a professional, but this has the disadvantage that one is less in touch with the actual research, so missing the excitement of the chase and, not least, the cost is apt to mount up.

Speaking of cost, it must be emphasised that there is absolutely no fixed relation between expenditure and results. A whole day may be spent in seeing a parish register and the search prove to be in vain – it may even be that a hoped-for entry is not there because there is a gap of a few years at the vital date, due to the forgetfulness of an 18th-century parson or parish clerk. It is, therefore, quite impossible to answer a question such as 'How much will it cost to trace my. family tree?'.

As stated at the start of Chapter 1 of this book, do remember to take the search back a step at a time, not leaping ahead to conclusions which may later prove to be wrong. It is much more satisfying to be sure of the links between one generation and the next than to produce an impressively long but tentative pedigree, riddled with question marks and dotted lines.

Finally, have fun, and enjoy the feeling of achievement as your knowledge of your ancestors increases.

A Bibliography for Beginners

General Guides

The Family Records Centre Introduction to Family History (1st edn. 1999)

A.J. Camp, *First Steps in Family History* (3rd edn. 1998)

G. Pelling, *Beginning Your Family History* (7th edn., 2001 updated by P. Litton)

J. Cole and J. Titford, *Tracing Your Family Tree* (3rd edn. 2000)

Recording Searches

I. Swinnerton, *Basic Approach to Keeping Family Records* (2nd edn., 1999)

M. Lynskey, *Family Trees: A Manual for their Design, Production and Display* (1996)

N. Bayley (comp.), *Computer Aided Genealogy: A Guide to Using Computer Software for Family History* (1998)

P. Christian, *Web Publishing for Genealogy* (2nd edn., 1999)

D. Hawgood, *An Introduction to Using Computers for Genealogy* (3rd edn., 2002)

Using the Internet

P. Christian, *The Genealogist's Internet* (reprinted 2002)

S.A. Raymond (comp.), *Family History on the Web: An Internet Directory for England and Wales* (2nd ed., 2002)

D. Hawgood, *Internet for Genealogy* (2nd edn., 1999)

C. Peacock, *The Good Web Guide to Genealogy* (2002)

Interpretation

R. Pols, *Genealogists' Guide to Family Photographs 1860-1945* (2002)

L. Munby, *Dates and Time: A Handbook* (1997)

E.E. Thoyts, *How to Read Old Documents* (reprinted 2001)

A. Ison, *The Secretary Hand 'ABC' Book* (2000)

S. Hobbs and L. Munby, *Reading Tudor and Stuart Handwriting* (2002)

W.S.B. Buck, *Examples of Handwriting 1550-1650* (reprinted 1996)

M. Gandy, *Basic Approach to Latin for Family Historians* (1995)

D. Stuart, *Latin for Local and Family Historians* (1995)

C.T. Martin, *The Record Interpreter* (reprinted 2002)

Civil Registration and Census Returns

S. Colwell, *The Family Records Centre: A User's Guide* (2002)

A. Collins, *Basic Facts about Using the Family Records Centre* (1997)

B. Langston, *Handbook to Civil Registration Districts of England and Wales* (2001)

S. Lumas, *Making Use of the Census* (4th edn., 2002)

J. Gibson and E. Hampson, *Census returns in Microform 1841-1891: A Directory to Local Holdings in Great Britain, Channel Islands and Isle of Man* (6th edn., 2001)

Parish Registers and Other Records

C.R. Humphery-Smith (ed.), *The Phillimore Atlas and Index of Parish Registers* (3rd edn., 2003)

L. Gibbens, *An Introduction to Church Registers* (1997)

J. Gibson and E. Hampson, *Marriage and Census Indexes for Family Historians* (8th edn., 2000)

A List of Parishes in Boyd's Marriage Index (reprinted 1994)

W.E. Tate, *The Parish Chest* (3rd edn., 1983)

A. Cole, *An Introduction to Poor Law Documents before 1834* (2nd edn., 2000)

N. Currer-Briggs and R. Gambier, *Huguenot Ancestry* (2001)

R. Wenzerul (ed.), *Jewish Ancestors? A Beginner's Guide* (2nd edn., 2001)

Society of Genealogists' booklets in the series *My Ancestors Were.....* on *Baptists, Congregationalists in England and Wales, English Presbyterians and Unitarians, Methodists, Quakers, Jewish, in the Salvation Army*

Federation of Family History Societies' *Basic Facts* guides on *Using Baptism Records, Using Marriage Records, English Nonconformity for Family Historians, Tracing Catholic Ancestry in England*

The National Archives/P.R.O. Pocket Guides to *Tracing Catholic Ancestors, Tracing Nonconformist Ancestors, Using Poor Law Records*

Wills

J. Gibson and E. Churchill, *Probate Jurisdictions: Where to Look for Wills* (5th edn., 2002)

Other Ecclesiastical Records

A. Tarver, *Church Court Records* (1994)

J. Gibson, *Bishops' Transcripts and Marriage Licences, Bonds and Allegations: A Guide to their Location and Indexes* (5th edn., 2001)

The National Archives: Public Record Office

A. Bevan (ed.), *Tracing Your Ancestors in the Public Record Office* (6th edn., 2002)

J. Cox, *New to Kew?* (2001)

The National Archives Information Leaflets as appropriate

S. Fowler and W. Spencer, *Army Records for Family Historians* (2nd edn.,1998)

B. Pappalardo, *Tracing Your Naval Ancestors* (2002)

W. Spencer, *Air Force Records for Family Historians* (2000)

K. Smith, C.T. Watts and M.J. Watts, *Records of Merchant Shipping and Seamen* (2001)

J. Gibson, M. Medlycott and D. Mills, *Land and Window Tax Assessments* (2nd edn., 1998)

The National Archives/P.R.O. Pocket Guides to *Using Army Records, Using Criminal Records, Using Navy Records*

Libraries and Record Offices

F.G. Emmison, *Introduction to Archives* (1977)

J. Gibson and P. Peskett, *Record Offices: How to Find Them* (9th ed., 2002)

J. Cole and R. Church, *In and Around Record Repositories in Great Britain and Ireland* (4th edn. 1998)

A. Collins, *Basic Facts about Using Colindale and other Newspaper Repositories* (2001)

V.E. Aldous, *My Ancestors were Freemen of the City of London* (1999)

J. Gibson and C. Rogers, *Coroners' Records in England and Wales* (2000)

Other Sources

J. Gibson and E. Hampson, *Specialist Indexes for Family Historians* (2nd edn., 2000)

D. Stuart, *Manorial Records* (1992)

P. Palgrave-Moore, *How to Locate and Use Manorial Records* (2nd edn., 1993)

M. Ellis, *Using Manorial Records* (2nd edn., 2001)

J. Gibson, B. Langston and B.W. Smith, *Local Newspapers 1759-1920: A Select Location List* (2nd edn., 2002)

S.A. Raymond, *Occupational Sources for Family Historians* (2nd edn., 1995)

C. Waters, *A Dictionary of Old Trades, Titles and Occupations* (2nd edn., 2002)

J. Cornwall, *An Introduction to Reading Old Title Deeds* (2nd edn. 1997)

N.W. Alcock, *Old Title Deeds* (2001)

P. Hindle, *Maps for Historians* (reprinted 2002)

E.J. Evans, *Tithes: Maps, Apportionments and the 1836 Act* (1997)

J. Unett and A. Tanner, *Making a Pedigree: An Introduction to Sources for Early Genealogy* (1997)

P. Franklin, *Some Medieval Records for Family Historians* (1994)

Wales, Scotland and Ireland

J. & S. Rowlands (ed.), *Welsh Family History: A Guide to Research* (2nd edn., 1998)

G.K. Hamilton-Edwards, *In Search of Scottish Ancestry* (2nd edn., 1983)

C. Sinclair, *Tracing your Scottish Ancestors in the Scottish Record Office* (1997)

B. Davis, *Irish Ancestry, A Beginner's Guide* (3rd edn., 2001)

J. Grenham, *Tracing Your Irish Ancestors* (2nd edn., 1999)

The National Archives/P.R.O. Pocket Guides to *Tracing Scottish Ancestors, Tracing Irish Ancestors*

Regnal Years

Dates in older manuscripts are often expressed by the regnal year. To be quite sure which year is referred to it is necessary to know the day of the year in which the reign officially began. For instance, the reign of Queen Elizabeth I began on 17 November 1558. From 17 November 1558 to 16 November 1559 was therefore the year 1 Eliz. The year 3 Eliz. would begin two years later, i.e. 17 November 1560. The year 34 Eliz. would begin 33 years later, i.e. on 17 November 1591.

There are in some cases short gaps between the official dates at the beginning of a new reign, but, apart from these and a complication in the reign of John, a simple calculation from the opening dates given below will enable a date expressed by regnal year to be identified.

Dates are not given here after the reign of Queen Victoria, as the regnal year is then practically only used for Acts of Parliament and in their case is expressed differently, as it must be related to the Parliamentary Session in which the Act is passed.

William I	25 Dec. 1066
William II	26 Sept. 1087
Henry I	5 Aug. 1100
Stephen	26 Dec. 1135
Henry II	19 Dec. 1154
Richard I	3 Sept. 1189
John*	27 May 1199
Henry III	28 Oct. 1216
Edward II	20 Nov. 1272
Edward II	8 July 1307
Edward III	25 Jan. 1327
Richard II	22 June 1377
Henry IV	30 Sept. 1399
Henry V	21 Mar. 1413
Henry VI	1 Sept. 1422
Edward IV	4 Mar. 1461

Edward V	9 Apr. 1483
Richard III	26 June 1483
Henry VII	22 Aug. 1485
Edward VI	28 Jan. 1547
Mary	6 July 1553
Philip and Mary	25 July 1554
Elizabeth I	17 Nov. 1558
James I	24 Mar. 1603
Charles I	27 Mar. 1625
Commonwealth†	
Charles II	30 Jan. 1649
James II	6 Feb. 1685
(Interregnum 12 Dec. 1688 to 12 Feb. 1689)	
William III and Mary	13 Feb. 1689
William III	28 Dec. 1694
Anne	8 Mar. 1702
George I	1 Aug. 1714
George II	11 June 1727
George III	25 Oct. 1760
George IV	29 Jan. 1820
William IV	26 June 1830
Victoria	20 June 1837

* In the case of John, regnal years are calculated from Ascension Day each year, which is a moveable feast in the calendar. For full details see *The Oxford Companion to English Literature*, Appendix IV.

† No regnal year was used during the Commonwealth 30 Jan. 1649 to 29 May 1660. On the Restoration the years of the reign of Charles II were dated from the death of Charles I on the principle that he had been King *de jure* since then.

The reader might like to be reminded here of the change in the method of dating which came into force in 1752 (see p.35).

It is also useful to know that early documents were dated by reference to the nearest festival of the church. A *Handbook of Dates* by C.R. Cheney gives all the saints' days and festivals. It also sets out all the regnal years with numbers referring to tables which provided calendars for each year.

A Foot of Fine

Note: The bold type and italics are the author's in an attempt to make the reading easier.

This is the final concord made in the Court of the Lady Queen at Westminster on the octave of the Purification of Blessed Mary (*Feb. 9*) in the eighth year of the reign of Anne (*1710*) by God's grace queen of Great Britain, France and Ireland, Defender of the Faith, etc. after the Conquest, in the presence of Thomas Trevor, John Blencoe, Robert Tracy and Robert Dormer, justices and other faithful subjects of the Lady Queen then present there, **between** *David Clarke, John Lampard, John Broadwood* and *James Mitchell,* plaintiffs **and** *Elizabeth* his wife, *Robert Crosse, Joan Broadway,* widow, and *William Mumford* and *Brigit* his wife, deforciants; **concerning** four messuages and three gardens with appurtenances in the City of Winchester, **whence a plea of agreement** was summoned between them in the same court, namely that the aforesaid James Crosse & Elizabeth, Robert, Joan & Brigit recognise that the aforesaid tenements with appurtenances are the right of David, as those which the same David, John, John and James Mitchell have by gift of the aforesaid James Crosse & Elizabeth, Joan & William & Brigit & their heirs to the aforesaid David, John, John & James Mitchell & the heirs of David for ever. **And furthermore** the same *James Crosse & Elizabeth* granted for themselves and the heirs of that James that they guarantee to the aforesaid David, John, John, & James Mitchell & David's heirs the aforesaid tenements with appurtenances against the aforesaid James Crosse and Elizabeth and James' heirs for ever. **And further** the same *Robert* granted for himself and his heirs that they guarantee to the aforesaid

David, John, John and James Mitchell & David's heirs the aforesaid tenements with appurtenances against the aforesaid Robert and his heirs for ever. **And in addition** the same *Joan* granted for herself and her heirs that they guarantee to the aforesaid David, John, John and James Mitchell & David's heirs the aforesaid tenements with appurtenances against the aforesaid Joan and her heirs for ever. **And also** the same *William* & *Brigit* granted for themselves and William's heirs that they guarantee to the aforesaid David, John, John & James Mitchell & David's heirs the aforesaid tenements with appurtenances against the aforesaid William & Brigit and William's heirs for ever. **And for this** recognition, remission, quit claim, guarantee, fine & concord the said David, John, John & James Mitchell gave the aforesaid James Crosse & Elizabeth, Robert, Joan & William *two hundred pounds sterling*.

The National Archives: Public Record Office CP 25 (2)/964, 8 Anne, Hilary. Translated from the Latin by the College of Arms.

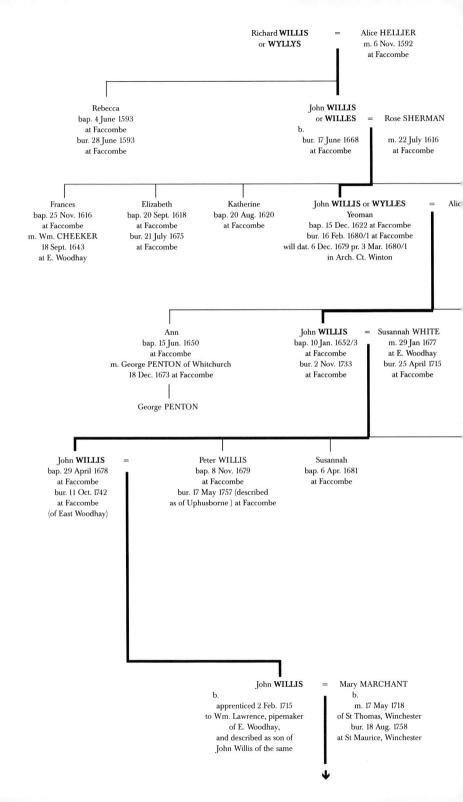

Richard **WILLIS**
or **WYLLYS**

= Alice HELLIER
m. 6 Nov. 1592
at Faccombe

Rebecca
bap. 4 June 1593
at Faccombe
bur. 28 June 1593
at Faccombe

John **WILLIS**
or **WILLES**
b.
bur. 17 June 1668
at Faccombe

= Rose SHERMAN

m. 22 July 1616
at Faccombe

Frances
bap. 25 Nov. 1616
at Faccombe
m. Wm. CHEEKER
18 Sept. 1643
at E. Woodhay

Elizabeth
bap. 20 Sept. 1618
at Faccombe
bur. 21 July 1675
at Faccombe

Katherine
bap. 20 Aug. 1620
at Faccombe

John **WILLIS** or **WYLLES**
Yeoman
bap. 15 Dec. 1622 at Faccombe
bur. 16 Feb. 1680/1 at Faccombe
will dat. 6 Dec. 1679 pr. 3 Mar. 1680/1
in Arch. Ct. Winton

= Alic

Ann
bap. 15 Jun. 1650
at Faccombe
m. George PENTON of Whitchurch
18 Dec. 1673 at Faccombe

John **WILLIS**
bap. 10 Jan. 1652/3
at Faccombe
bur. 2 Nov. 1733
at Faccombe

= Susannah WHITE
m. 29 Jan 1677
at E. Woodhay
bur. 25 April 1715
at Faccombe

George PENTON

John **WILLIS**
bap. 29 April 1678
at Faccombe
bur. 11 Oct. 1742
at Faccombe
(of East Woodhay)

=

Peter WILLIS
bap. 8 Nov. 1679
at Faccombe
bur. 17 May 1757 (described
as of Uphusborne) at Faccombe

Susannah
bap. 6 Apr. 1681
at Faccombe

John **WILLIS**
b.
apprenticed 2 Feb. 1715
to Wm. Lawrence, pipemaker
of E. Woodhay,
and described as son of
John Willis of the same

= Mary MARCHANT
b.
m. 17 May 1718
of St Thomas, Winchester
bur. 18 Aug. 1758
at St Maurice, Winchester

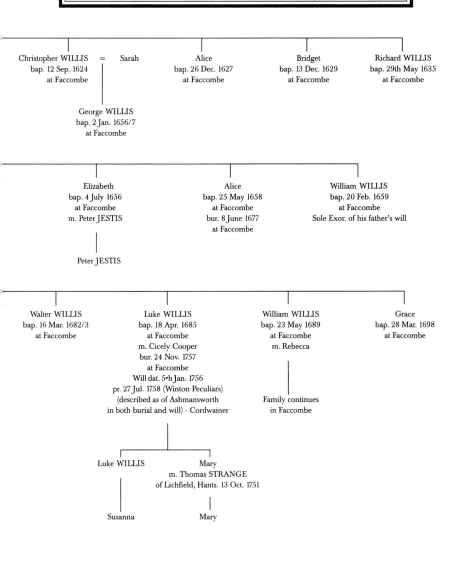

THE FAMILY OF
WILLIS
OF FACCOMBE AND WINCHESTER, HANTS.,
AND EALING, MIDDLESEX

Christopher WILLIS = Sarah
bap. 12 Sep. 1624
at Faccombe

Alice
bap. 26 Dec. 1627
at Faccombe

Bridget
bap. 13 Dec. 1629
at Faccombe

Richard WILLIS
bap. 29th May 1635
at Faccombe

George WILLIS
bap. 2 Jan. 1656/7
at Faccombe

Elizabeth
bap. 4 July 1656
at Faccombe
m. Peter JESTIS

Alice
bap. 25 May 1658
at Faccombe
bur. 8 June 1677
at Faccombe

William WILLIS
bap. 20 Feb. 1659
at Faccombe
Sole Exor. of his father's will

Peter JESTIS

Walter WILLIS
bap. 16 Mar. 1682/3
at Faccombe

Luke WILLIS
bap. 18 Apr. 1685
at Faccombe
m. Cicely Cooper
bur. 24 Nov. 1757
at Faccombe
Will dat. 5•h Jan. 1756
pr. 27 Jul. 1758 (Winton Peculiars)
(described as of Ashmansworth
in both burial and will) - Cordwainer

William WILLIS
bap. 23 May 1689
at Faccombe
m. Rebecca

Family continues
in Faccombe

Grace
bap. 28 Mar. 1698
at Faccombe

Luke WILLIS

Mary
m. Thomas STRANGE
of Lichfield, Hants. 13 Oct. 1751

Susanna

Mary

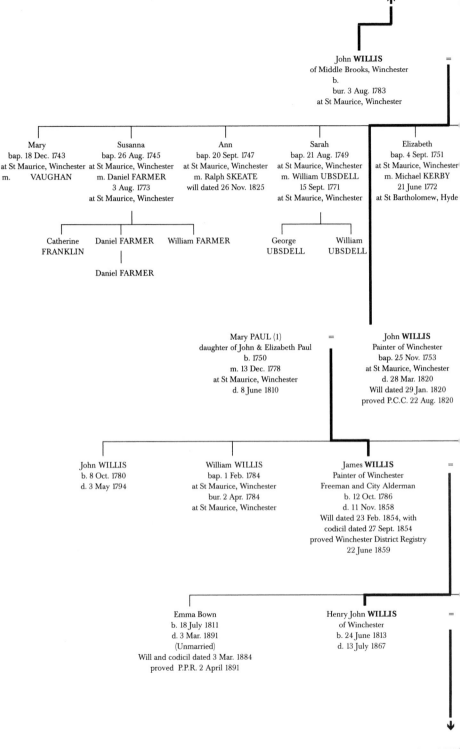

John **WILLIS**
of Middle Brooks, Winchester
b.
bur. 3 Aug. 1783
at St Maurice, Winchester
=

Mary
bap. 18 Dec. 1743
at St Maurice, Winchester
m.   VAUGHAN

Susanna
bap. 26 Aug. 1745
at St Maurice, Winchester
m. Daniel FARMER
3 Aug. 1773
at St Maurice, Winchester

Ann
bap. 20 Sept. 1747
at St Maurice, Winchester
m. Ralph SKEATE
will dated 26 Nov. 1825

Sarah
bap. 21 Aug. 1749
at St Maurice, Winchester
m. William UBSDELL
15 Sept. 1771
at St Maurice, Winchester

Elizabeth
bap. 4 Sept. 1751
at St Maurice, Winchester
m. Michael KERBY
21 June 1772
at St Bartholomew, Hyde

Catherine
FRANKLIN

Daniel FARMER

William FARMER

Daniel FARMER

George
UBSDELL

William
UBSDELL

Mary PAUL (1)
daughter of John & Elizabeth Paul
b. 1750
m. 13 Dec. 1778
at St Maurice, Winchester
d. 8 June 1810

=

John **WILLIS**
Painter of Winchester
bap. 25 Nov. 1753
at St Maurice, Winchester
d. 28 Mar. 1820
Will dated 29 Jan. 1820
proved P.C.C. 22 Aug. 1820

John WILLIS
b. 8 Oct. 1780
d. 3 May 1794

William WILLIS
bap. 1 Feb. 1784
at St Maurice, Winchester
bur. 2 Apr. 1784
at St Maurice, Winchester

James **WILLIS**
Painter of Winchester
Freeman and City Alderman
b. 12 Oct. 1786
d. 11 Nov. 1858
Will dated 23 Feb. 1854, with
codicil dated 27 Sept. 1854
proved Winchester District Registry
22 June 1859

=

Emma Bown
b. 18 July 1811
d. 3 Mar. 1891
(Unmarried)
Will and codicil dated 3 Mar. 1884
proved P.P.R. 2 April 1891

Henry John **WILLIS**
of Winchester
b. 24 June 1813
d. 13 July 1867

=

James WILL

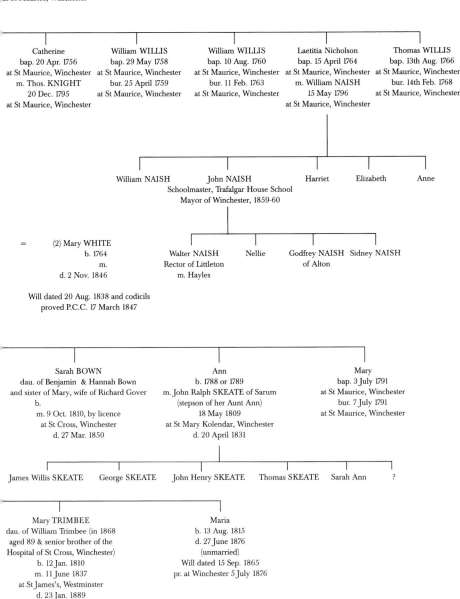

Mary RUMNEY
b.
m. 25 July 1743
at St Maurice, Winchester

Catherine	William WILLIS	William WILLIS	Laetitia Nicholson	Thomas WILLIS
bap. 20 Apr. 1756	bap. 29 May 1758	bap. 10 Aug. 1760	bap. 15 April 1764	bap. 13th Aug. 1766
at St Maurice, Winchester	at St Maurice, Winchester	at St Maurice, Winchester	at St Maurice, Winchester	at St Maurice, Winchester
m. Thos. KNIGHT	bur. 25 April 1759	bur. 11 Feb. 1763	m. William NAISH	bur. 14th Feb. 1768
20 Dec. 1795	at St Maurice, Winchester	at St Maurice, Winchester	15 May 1796	at St Maurice, Winchester
at St Maurice, Winchester			at St Maurice, Winchester	

William NAISH	John NAISH	Harriet	Elizabeth	Anne
	Schoolmaster, Trafalgar House School			
	Mayor of Winchester, 1859-60			

= (2) Mary WHITE
b. 1764
m.
d. 2 Nov. 1846

Walter NAISH	Nellie	Godfrey NAISH	Sidney NAISH
Rector of Littleton		of Alton	
m. Hayles			

Will dated 20 Aug. 1838 and codicils
proved P.C.C. 17 March 1847

Sarah BOWN	Ann	Mary
dau. of Benjamin & Hannah Bown	b. 1788 or 1789	bap. 3 July 1791
and sister of Mary, wife of Richard Gover	m. John Ralph SKEATE of Sarum	at St Maurice, Winchester
b.	(stepson of her Aunt Ann)	bur. 7 July 1791
m. 9 Oct. 1810, by licence	18 May 1809	at St Maurice, Winchester
at St Cross, Winchester	at St Mary Kolendar, Winchester	
d. 27 Mar. 1850	d. 20 April 1831	

James Willis SKEATE	George SKEATE	John Henry SKEATE	Thomas SKEATE	Sarah Ann	?

Mary TRIMBEE	Maria
dau. of William Trimbee (in 1868	b. 13 Aug. 1815
aged 89 & senior brother of the	d. 27 June 1876
Hospital of St Cross, Winchester)	(unmarried)
b. 12 Jan. 1810	Will dated 15 Sep. 1865
m. 11 June 1837	pr. at Winchester 5 July 1876
at St James's, Westminster	
d. 23 Jan. 1889	

Sarah Elizabeth
b. 28 June 1837
m. Richard SNOW
Miller, of Abbotsworthy, Winchester
25 Jan. 1865
at St Peter, Cheesehill, Winchester

James Herbert **WILLIS** L.R.I.B.A.   =   Annie Elizabeth PAPAZOGLU
Architect, H.M. Office of Works   dau. of George & Sarah Papazoglu
of Ealing, Middlesex and the   b. 13 Aug. 1871
British Embassy, Constantinople   m. 29 Jan. 1894
b. 4 March 1864   at British Consulate General and
d. 15 Dec. 1950   Constantinople
Will dated 17 Nov. 1944 and   d. 24 Mar. 1939
codicil dated 14 Mar. 1947
proved P.P.R. 24 Jan. 1951

Arthur James **WILLIS** F.R.I.C.S.   =   Audrey Isabel Edith Thompson
Chartered Quantity Surveyor   dau. of Thomas Moore-Lane and
of Ealing, Middlesex and   Isabel Mary THOMPSON of Ealing
Lyminge, Kent   b. 5 July 1897
b. 16 Jan. 1895   m. at St John's, Ealing
at Constantinople   3 Aug. 1918
d. 26 Nov. 1983   d. 29 Sept. 1981

Cicely Mary   =   John Norman CAPENER   Christopher James **WILLIS** F.R.I.C.S.
B.A. (Lond.)   M.A. (Cantab.), M.I.C.E.   b. 25 May 1928
b. 29 Nov. 1922   son of Norman Capener, F.R.C.S.   at Ealing, Middlesex
m. Lyminge, Kent   of Exeter, Devon
17 June 1950   b. 23 Aug. 1924

James Andrew **WILLIS**   =   Moira Patricia   Jane Rosemary
B.Sc., F.R.I.C.S.,   dau. of Dermot   b. 28 Jan. 1959
Dip.Arb., A.C.I.Arb   James and   d. 28 Jan. 1960
Chartered Quantity Surveyor   Eileen RUSSELL
of New Malden, Surrey   b. 28 May 1957
b. 2 Oct. 1957   m. 15 Oct. 1983

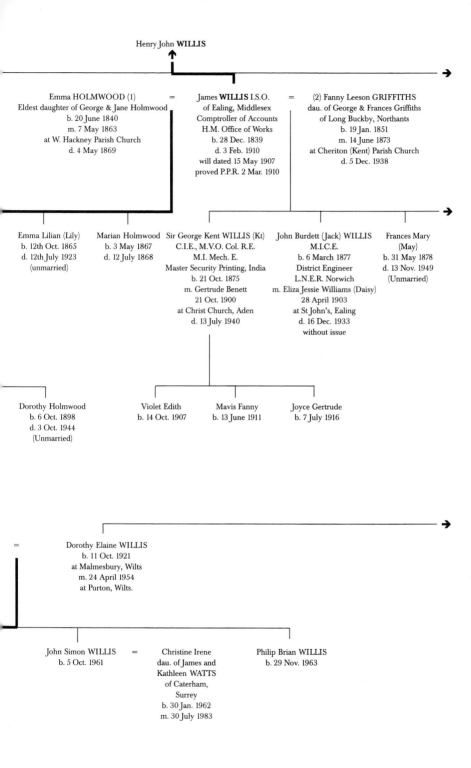

Henry John **WILLIS**

Emma HOLMWOOD (1)
Eldest daughter of George & Jane Holmwood
b. 20 June 1840
m. 7 May 1863
at W. Hackney Parish Church
d. 4 May 1869

= James **WILLIS** I.S.O.
of Ealing, Middlesex
Comptroller of Accounts
H.M. Office of Works
b. 28 Dec. 1839
d. 3 Feb. 1910
will dated 15 May 1907
proved P.P.R. 2 Mar. 1910

= (2) Fanny Leeson GRIFFITHS
dau. of George & Frances Griffiths
of Long Buckby, Northants
b. 19 Jan. 1851
m. 14 June 1873
at Cheriton (Kent) Parish Church
d. 5 Dec. 1938

Emma Lilian (Lily)
b. 12th Oct. 1865
d. 12th July 1923
(unmarried)

Marian Holmwood
b. 3 May 1867
d. 12 July 1868

Sir George Kent WILLIS (Kt)
C.I.E., M.V.O. Col. R.E.
M.I. Mech. E.
Master Security Printing, India
b. 21 Oct. 1875
m. Gertrude Benett
21 Oct. 1900
at Christ Church, Aden
d. 13 July 1940

John Burdett (Jack) WILLIS
M.I.C.E.
b. 6 March 1877
District Engineer
L.N.E.R. Norwich
m. Eliza Jessie Williams (Daisy)
28 April 1903
at St John's, Ealing
d. 16 Dec. 1933
without issue

Frances Mary
(May)
b. 31 May 1878
d. 13 Nov. 1949
(Unmarried)

Dorothy Holmwood
b. 6 Oct. 1898
d. 3 Oct. 1944
(Unmarried)

Violet Edith
b. 14 Oct. 1907

Mavis Fanny
b. 13 June 1911

Joyce Gertrude
b. 7 July 1916

= Dorothy Elaine WILLIS
b. 11 Oct. 1921
at Malmesbury, Wilts
m. 24 April 1954
at Purton, Wilts.

John Simon WILLIS
b. 5 Oct. 1961

= Christine Irene
dau. of James and
Kathleen WATTS
of Caterham,
Surrey
b. 30 Jan. 1962
m. 30 July 1983

Philip Brian WILLIS
b. 29 Nov. 1963

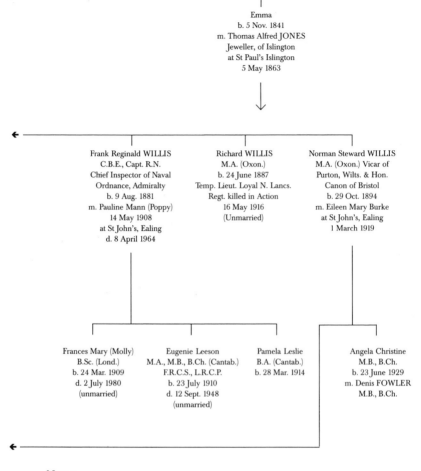

Emma
b. 5 Nov. 1841
m. Thomas Alfred JONES
Jeweller, of Islington
at St Paul's Islington
5 May 1863

Frank Reginald WILLIS
C.B.E., Capt. R.N.
Chief Inspector of Naval
Ordnance, Admiralty
b. 9 Aug. 1881
m. Pauline Mann (Poppy)
14 May 1908
at St John's, Ealing
d. 8 April 1964

Richard WILLIS
M.A. (Oxon.)
b. 24 June 1887
Temp. Lieut. Loyal N. Lancs.
Regt. killed in Action
16 May 1916
(Unmarried)

Norman Steward WILLIS
M.A. (Oxon.) Vicar of
Purton, Wilts. & Hon.
Canon of Bristol
b. 29 Oct. 1894
m. Eileen Mary Burke
at St John's, Ealing
1 March 1919

Frances Mary (Molly)
B.Sc. (Lond.)
b. 24 Mar. 1909
d. 2 July 1980
(unmarried)

Eugenie Leeson
M.A., M.B., B.Ch. (Cantab.)
F.R.C.S., L.R.C.P.
b. 23 July 1910
d. 12 Sept. 1948
(unmarried)

Pamela Leslie
B.A. (Cantab.)
b. 28 Mar. 1914

Angela Christine
M.B., B.Ch.
b. 23 June 1929
m. Denis FOWLER
M.B., B.Ch.

Notes:

Richard Wyllys appears in the Court Roll of Faccombe Manor, 22 October 1952 and 22 March 1592/3 as excused from service as juror (B.M. Add. Ch.5070, 5072)

Burials at Faccombe: Alice Willis, 29 July 1646. Alice Willis, 23 July 1673 (2 burials for 3 Alices–? which).

John Willis m. Margerie Waterman at Linkenholt, 9 October 1637. ? second marriage of John m. Rose Sherman. No issue found at Linkenholt.

A Luke Willis was buried at St Maurice, Winchester, 2 January 1780. He may have been son of Luke of Ashmansworth (buried 1757) at Faccombe.

The burial of John Willis in 1742, assumed to be that of John (born 1678), might be that of John the pipe-maker (married 1718). There is a burial of a John Willis at Hamstead Marshall 18 December 1715, which might be that of John (born 1678).

Index

Page numbers in **bold** refer to illustrations

NOTES

NOTES

NOTES

NOTES

NOTES

NOTES